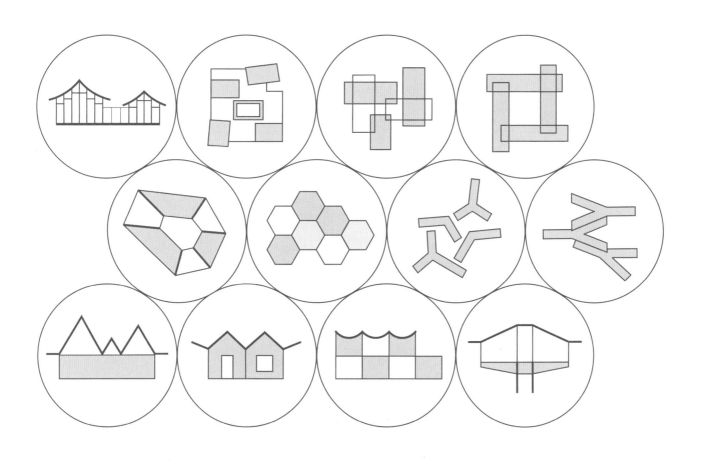

REBIRTH OF FORM-TYPE

Selected Works of

SCENIC ARCHITECTURE OFFICE

Zhu Xiaofeng

CONTENTS

004
The Dialectical Architecture of Zhu Xiaofeng
Kenneth Frampton

010
The Integration of Thought and Practice
Wu Jiang

012
From Jiangnan Aesthetics to an Architecture of Embodiment
— The Practice of Scenic Architecture Office
Li Xiangning

018
Rebirth of Form-type
Zhu Xiaofeng

APPENDIX

291
Project Chronology 2004–2021

293
Scenic Architecture Office

295
Distinctions

296
Exhibitions

297
Lectures

299
Publications

303
Staff Appreciation

304
Image Credits

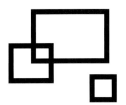

COURTYARD SETTLEMENT

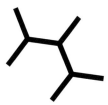

FREE CELL

EXTENSION OF HOME

024

Reviving Courtyards in a Historic Neighborhood
Shengli Street Neighborhood Committee and Senior Citizens' Daycare Center

112

Scene Collector
Community Pavilion at Jintao Village

200

Folded Plates Take-off
Activity Homes at Yunjin Road

042

Convergence of Frames
Zhujiajiao Museum of Humanities and Arts

128

Childhood in a Honeycomb
Bilingual Kindergarten Affiliated to East China Normal University

224

Rainbow Hung from Cornice
Bridge of Nine Terraces

066

A Tree of Terraces
Lattice Book House

152

Floating Among Trees
Shanghai Google Creators' Society Center

242

Interwoven Auras
Dongyuan Qianxun Community Center

086

Interactive Platforms
Pudong Adolescent Activity Center and Civic Art Center

180

Enlightenment of Waves
Dashawan Beach Facility at Lianyungang

264

Collaborating with Nature
Deep Dive Rowing Club

Kenneth Frampton   Architect, historian, and critic
Ware Professor of Architecture, Graduate School of Architecture,
Planning and Preservation, Columbia University

THE DIALECTICAL ARCHITECTURE OF ZHU XIAOFENG

After he finished his graduate studies at Harvard, Zhu Xiaofeng returned to his native Shanghai and founded the practice of Scenic Architecture Office. Three years later, in 2007, he established the point of departure for the practice with a remarkable work that combined the traditional gable roof of the region with the quintessentially modern concept of spatial interpenetration. This project was Shengli Street Neighborhood Committee and Senior Citizens' Daycare Center, which he realized in the canal town of Zhujiajiao (the Venice of Shanghai) in 2008. The highly contextual character of this work depends not only on the double-pitched, curved profile of the traditional gable roof, but also on its necessary stepped timber frame, as well as the projecting cylindrical purlins integral to the form. This traditional character is augmented by the cylindrical, slightly tapered timber columns supporting the roof, and by the full-height timber mullions and vertical louvers that establish the two-and-a-half roof façade facing the canal. This format is complemented by a proliferation of full-height lattice-work pivoting timber doors that separate the senior citizens' canteen and recreation room from the principal courtyard established by four monumental columns set at the four corners of the space.

By the time Scenic Architecture Office took on this project, two tropes were already characteristic of the practice: a labyrinthine juxtaposition of cellular space that, as far as possible, dispenses with corridors, and second, a highly disciplined approach adopted toward the building method, in which elements are detailed in a manner that is at once both technically inventive and aesthetically effective.

This dualistic precept was already evident in the practice's earlier works; first, in the articulation of the timber roofwork, derived directly from the southern Yangtze River Delta tradition, and second, by virtue of the specific sequence adopted in the cladding of the roof—a conventional brick tile for the exposed soffit, accompanied by the prerequisite insulation and waterproof layer, before being finished in the traditional black tile of the region.

Scenic Architecture Office's penchant for the labyrinthic discretely manifests itself in three works designed and realized for the Shanghai region over 2008 to 2016. The first of these is Zhujiajiao Museum of Humanities and Arts; the second is Lattice Book House; and the third is a youth and children's center combined with an arts center for the Pudong New District (Pudong Adolescent Activity Center and Civic Art Center).

Built on a verdant site, close to a disused rail line, with a view over the water, Lattice Book House is a constructive technological tour de force in steel, wherein four steel lattice platforms are carried on eleven welded steel lattices that pinwheel around a set of central switch-back stairs to support a sequence of pinwheeling cantilevered steel lattice decks and roof planes. What is an extremely dematerialized work in steel—made out of thin stainless-steel profiles framing large glass upstands and aluminum window frames—is otherwise finished in bamboo. Apart from the stainless-steel balustrades, which are filled with 0.8-inch (20-millimeter) stainless-steel mesh and full-height floor-to-floor plate glass panels framed in aluminum, this work is otherwise finished with a warm, natural material: bamboo flooring and a 0.8-inch (20-millimeter) deep, louvered bamboo ceiling. The edges of the 17.7-inch (450-millimter) cantilevered planes are also faced in timber, as are the exposed upper surfaces of the stairs. The vertical space-dividing steel lattice panels are painted with dark-gray polyurethane acrylic paints. The other exceptional aspect of this invention and perfection of an unprecedented, largely prefabricated, dry building system is the integration of all the electro-mechanical services, drainage, and such, within the depth of the steel lattice work. Inspired by Dutch Neoplasticism on the one hand, and the postwar works of Ludwig Mies van der Rohe on the other—not to mention, a certain subtle influence coming from Japanese minimalism—this building, with its principal out-riding roof terraces facing southeast and southwest, looking over the water and the high-rise city, is, in fact, a belvedere from which to enjoy the flora of the well-established park grove in which it is embedded; one also enjoys the largely empty, part ornamental, part structural, floor-to-ceiling, lattice-work bookshelves in steel that articulate the continuity of the space. Lattice Book House has become another increasingly familiar new destination for Chinese youth—a place that a relatively affluent generation of the People's Republic visit often to simultaneously hang out, "meditate," bask in nature, and occasionally listen to informal lectures given at the top of the stairs. Up to now, books qua books seem to be only incidental, decorative-cum-evocative elements, suspended here and there in the lattice-work steel screens that rotate freely about the nexus of the central stairs.

The next work of consequence in the sequence of works that Scenic Architecture Office records is the combined Pudong Adolescent Activity Center and Civic Art Center in Pudong New District, Shanghai. Conceived as the logical extension of the Lattice Book House, the Pudong Adolescent Activity Center and Civic Art Center—as an integrally serviced steel platform carried on a regular grid of box steel columns, and the occasional Y-shaped composite column—depends on the open-ended, partially top-lit "space-frame" character of its form for its success. The description provided by the office succinctly describes the overall strategy underlying the design:

Two interlocked courtyard structures are composed by the platforms. The auditorium, with a seating capacity of 1,000, and the Civic Art Center are located at the western ring connected to the metro plaza, while the Adolescent Activity Center is located on the eastern, which is surrounded by green land. By overlapping and linking with each other, the platforms stimulate interactions between different areas and programs. The garden platform spanning across the river links the two lobbies of both sides and becomes the spine of the public flow. With various indoor and outdoor spaces on the platforms, from the second to the fourth floors, the design frees the ground space to provide an open zone between the library and the urban planning center, forming a pedestrian hub for the whole community.

When I first became aware of Scenic Architecture Office, I was immediately struck by the overtly constructivist character of their Dashawan Beach Facility that is built on one of the islands of Lianyungang set in the middle of the Chinese coastline. Built in the short space of two years, between 2007 and 2009, this spectacular overlapping series of inclined concrete platforms cascade down from a high ridge toward an expansive, luxurious, fine sand beach. This is, by any standards, an extraordinarily courageous and spectacular vision, which the young practice has realized with exceptional aplomb and confidence.

In essence, this project features another "platform" scheme, only now, the platforms are sometimes 13 feet (4 meters) deep and house accommodations, while at other times, they are alternatively sloping roofs, the whole being a sequence of retaining walls set against the severe rock face of a mountain; the platforms are elements varying in depth, running from a single floor to three floors. With exceptional ingenuity, each "thick" platform has a view over the ocean, so that the various restaurants, cafeterias, and bars built into the mass-form have views over the ocean. Reinforced-concrete has been selected as the ubiquitous material that constructs this "klein bottle" earthwork/roofwork. At the same time, the syntax of the detailing is consistently constructivist throughout, ranging from wire mesh and stainless-steel balustrading, to cylindrical pilotis, not forgetting the curtain walling of the concrete tower that crowns the composition as a belvedere-cum-restaurant. This tectonic language is extended into the interior, with the fenestration alternating between large areas of full-height steel-framed plate glass and equally full-height glass block walls that face corridors or the shower facilities. The practice's description openly declares the sensuous intent informing the use of this material. As the architects put it:

The exterior walls of the shower room are double-layered glass brick walls, which not only offer sufficient daylight, but also give privacy and joy to the shower experience. The interior walls are also double-

layered, with shower pipes in between. Hot and humid air is ventilated out through the high windows or the cavern above.

Two other equally tactile but decidedly opaque materials complete the spectrum of expression in the extensive decking and finish of the flat, inclined roof planes which proliferate throughout the work—namely, either well-tended greensward areas planted on earth and held in place by the concrete super structure, or anti-corrosion timber decking suspended on metal joists above a complex of insulation and waterproofing set on top of a concrete slab. In many respects, this extraordinary panoramic scheme may be seen as an ultra-modern elaborate extension of the esplanade-cum-boardwalk language of the nineteenth-century spa and seafront traditions. At the same time, aside from earlier avant gardist references, it is also a work that is, however inadvertently so, surely indebted to Tadao Ando's Awaji Yumebutai complex built on a ravaged site. And there is also, as always is the case with Scenic Architecture Office, an overt or covert reference to nature. As the practice explains: "What we learn from the sea is the vitality of the waves—they are chasing and overlapping with each other endlessly. To put this dynamism into the design, we create three Y-shaped units that are freely stacked, and which stretch out three-dimensionally." Herein lies an unexpected echo of the late eighteenth-century French concept of *architecture parlante*.

The extreme tension between universal modernity and Yangtze traditions is at times left indulgently unresolved through a labyrinthic arbitrary juxtaposition of space cells which have an overwhelmingly decorative character. This is seen in a series of layered, topographic roofworks, as we find this trope returned to in a sequence of closely interrelated projects, beginning with the brilliant Activity Homes at Yunjin Road (2014/2018), going on to Dongyuan Qianxun Community Center (2016/2017). This line ends in the Deep Dive Rowing Club, realized over 2016 to 2017.

In the Yunjin Road project, the activity homes—inseparable as a built fabric from a linear park established on the site of a disused airport runway on the west bank of the Shanghai Huangpu River—are public facilities comprising three separate structures: a coffee shop close to the metro, a community pavilion, and a restaurant, all employing virtually the same "folded plate" structural system. The most immediately striking aspect of this work is the way in which the module of the structure is rhythmically integrated with the module of the landscape planting, and how they are both part of the same linear continuity. Beyond this—in the practice's typical style—the folded plate roof-system is a coherent building system broken up into four distinct components: relatively deep reinforced-concrete earthwork, flexibly disposed 7.9-inch (200-millimeter) concrete shear walls, lattice steel truss work—variously spanning between the walls—and a composite pitched roof system of titanium-zinc sheet, with standing seams integrated with the truss work, and insulated and finished with a plaster board soffit.

Every so often, a half-module of the folded plate is introduced, so as to syncopate the cross section against the insistent linearity of the general system, which is additionally inflected through the cantilevered overhangs at the outer limits of the folded plates. The integration of the landscaping greensward or densely planted low shrubs and flower beds is an equally consummate aspect of the entire scheme. The use of low-E glass throughout, both for the skylight and the fenestration in general, is also a compelling feature, as is the hardwood flooring and wood-framed windows—both of which provide a discernible warmth and grace to the multiuse interior. One of the most intelligent provisions in this single-story system is the integration of the necessary air-conditioning ducts and equipment into the continuous section of the deep concrete earthwork/foundation on which the buildings are grounded. The varied steel-framed fenestration of the "sliding" gable end of the folded plates is an exceptionally ludic iteration, both without and within, along with the varied overruns of the steel truss roofs at the end of each building. By any standard, this is a late-modern masterwork of exceptional caliber, as much for its logical and technically elegant design, as for its aesthetically effective composition, which in conjunction with the landscape borders on the elegiac.

The one work which finally reveals the unmistakable presence of Louis I.Kahn's Kimbell that lies behind all these works, and which is roofed by some version of folded plate construction is the Dongyuan Qianxun Community Center, built within a left-over corner site in the canal city of Suzhou, which is otherwise renowned for its labyrinthic mixture of historical gardens and courtyard houses. Instead of folded plates, this building, designed to provide communal services to the adjacent row housing, is covered by inverted reinforced-concrete barrel roofs. Once again—as in the previous works mentioned—freely disposed gable walls serve to support the shallow inverted concrete vaults, the structure being designed so in order to be of sufficient depth and strength to carry the longest span.

According to the architects, the external profile of this sequence of wave-like gable walls is intended to evoke the omnipresence of water, and to hark back to the traditional architectural style of the southeast Yangtze River Delta. Ribbed, galvanized metal sheets cover the inverted vaults in such a fashion as to create a continuous gutter on the axis of the vault, in which rainwater is gathered.

If the Dongyuan Community Center is the one work of the office that has been most directly influenced by Kahn's Kimbell, then Deep Dive Rowing Club, built close to the center of Shanghai, amid the young forested landscape of Century Park in Pudong New District, is their first work to refer to post-Hugo Alvar Henrik Aalto Finnish-generation exfoliated architecture of say, Erkki A. Kairamo, Juha I. Leiviskä, and Pekka Helin. As in the Yunjin Road complex, here, too, multiple roofs are the primary expressive elements. At this point, Zhu Xiaofeng's architecture seems to refer, mostly incidentally, to Gottfried Semper's *Four Elements of Architecture* of 1851, wherein Semper gave priority to the basic opposition, as it were, between the roof work and the earthwork—although here, building quite literally in the water, the latter should, perhaps, more correctly be seen as "the waterwork;" the twin tubular steel six-pile structure, in two clusters, anchors the steel-framed cantilevered structure of the main building into the riverbed. Subsequently, the main roof over the rowing machine exercise shed gives rise to a parallel layered sequence of secondary, shallow-pitched, steel-framed roofs, which cover the entry, the locker, and the shower rooms. The asymmetrical, double pitch of these layered roofs give rise to an equally layered sequence of asymmetrical, free-standing canoe sheds, carried on thin tubular steel frames.

Here, we encounter a literal progressive exfoliation of the main roof out into the forest. A similar dematerialization also takes place underfoot, in the form of the stainless-steel grilled walkways between the canoe sheds, which are elegantly poised on concrete blocks on the grassland to allow plants and small animals to coexist with the regular human movement of unloading and carrying canoes to the water beneath the lines of free-standing sheds interlaced with the forest, as both peter out at the river's edge. The final coda to this symphonic assembly is the boarded timber sun deck, ramp, and launching platforms that extend out across the surface of the river, in strong contrast to the titanium-zinc roofs with their standing seams and the primary tubular steel work painted white, along with the soffits of the various sheds. This sets a chromatic symphony of gray roofing and white soffits against the green of the forest.

It is fitting that the first decade and a half of Scenic Architecture Office's practice should culminate in a lightweight steel-framed work of such a sublime ecological character. This elegant masterwork, ushers to a fitting crescendo, this point of Zhu's career. He is an architect who never lets his readers, nor his clients, forget that he is a professional who is equally dedicated to both the potential poetry and technical efficiency of all forms of appropriate construction, and that he sees the field as simultaneously located at the double dialectical interface between nature and culture in first instance, and between present and past in the second, and vice versa.

Wu Jiang

Vice President and Professor of Architecture, Tongji University
Academician, French Academy of Architecture
Vice President, ARCASIA (Architects Regional Council Asia)

Translator: Clemens Ruben

THE INTEGRATION OF THOUGHT AND PRACTICE

Scenic Architecture Office was founded by Zhu Xiaofeng shortly after his return from Harvard University's Graduate School of Design in 2004. He soon made a name for himself among architectural circles in China and abroad with his innovative works that incorporate the architectural and landscape characteristics of China's Jiangnan region, an area that lies south of the Yangtze River. Zhu has since continued to innovate with a series of works, becoming an important representative of the contemporary Chinese architectural movement dubbed the "New Jiangnan" style. I first became acquainted with his work at the Zhujiajiao Museum of Humanities and Arts, and was immediately impressed by his clear, simple, and highly modern "New Jiangnan" design. I have always felt that exploring the combination of tradition and modernity is an incredibly promising path in contemporary architecture, and for me, the Zhujiajiao Museum of Humanities and Arts is a piece that meets this criterion perfectly.

Just as I was expecting more of his works to further build on this style, Zhu stunned the Chinese architectural world once again in 2012 with a completely different direction. Suspended among trees, the Shanghai Google Creators' Society Center took his fame to higher rungs, both at home and overseas. I have the strong feeling that Zhu is not an architect who only sticks to a one-dimensional practice, nor does he care about the "style" that is attributed to him by the industry. The moment he finds inspiration in a specific setting, he will willingly discard the formal language he is known for. In my opinion, this is a professional quality that truly exceptional architects ought to possess, yet only few can actually obtain.

I later discovered that Zhu is also a very thoughtful architect. In his design process, he often reflects on the philosophical logic hidden within his works. He is not only concerned with the physical significance of architecture, but also—or even more so—with its metaphysical dimension. By chance, he became my doctoral student, which allowed us to discuss the theoretical questions of architecture together. It also gave me the opportunity to track his artistic thinking through his works, while at the same time explore the essential ontological issues of contemporary architecture. In most of our academic discussions, the relationship between architecture and humans is often seated at the very center. We firmly believe that without people, architecture has no meaning. But also, what would happen to people without architecture?

So, what exactly does architecture mean to humanity?

Zhu's thoughts, which reflect architecture as an extension of humanity, have become progressively clearer over the years. Following his thinking, architecture has become a part of both the human body and the mind.

In Zhu's own words, "The present is ripe with uncertainty." Humankind is facing not only unprecedented challenges, but also infinite possibilities brought about by rapid technological progress. The role of architecture in addressing these challenges seems to be diminishing, and traditional architecture appears to be losing its philosophical meaning. Our living environment is increasingly bound by the structures we have built—from which we cannot escape. And the environment that humans have created is increasingly shaping humanity itself. A renewed understanding of the ontology and essence of architecture can not only help architects understand the meaning of their profession and better respond to current challenges, but also help humankind truly understand the interdependence, interaction, and community that exists between humans and their living environment.

Precisely with this kind of thinking, Zhu's architectural practice liberates itself from various constraints and enters a state of relative freedom. Be it in the Bilingual Kindergarten Affiliated to East China Normal University or in the Pudong Adolescent Activity Center and Civic Art Center, we can directly experience his unrestrained handling of architectural forms and open-minded shaping of structural spaces. It is there that architecture fully exerts its importance, as an "extension of humans."

For this book, Zhu has selected twelve representative works, which not only demonstrate his exploration of architectural design over the past ten years, but which also represent his thoughts on the essence of architecture in the course of his practice. It is worth noting that this collection was completed almost simultaneously with his doctoral dissertation titled "Architecture as Extension of Human: Studies on Three Fundamental Paths of Architectural Evolution." In his thesis, his theoretical thinking and design practice are intertwined and mutually reinforcing, which is extremely rare for an architect. As his PhD advisor, I am overjoyed and proud of Zhu's achievements and I wish him a long and distinguished professional and academic career ahead!

Li Xiangning Dean, College of Architecture and Urban Planning, Tongji University *Translator: Clemens Ruben*
Professor and doctoral supervisor in architecture
Critic and curator
Editor-in-chief, *Architecture China*

FROM JIANGNAN AESTHETICS TO AN ARCHITECTURE OF EMBODIMENT
— The Practice of Scenic Architecture Office

Modern China witnessed nearly forty years of rapid development that was accompanied by a sense of self-criticism that emerged among contemporary Chinese architects, which gradually helped pave a clear path in their architectural practice. During this time, two distinctly different tangents evolved among China's architectural practices. One was the transplantation and transformation of Western modernist architectural language, and the attempt to compensate for China's belated modernist enlightenment; this trend manifested itself in the new wave of research into, and interpretation of, the works of modernist masters such as Le Corbusier, Louis I. Kahn, and Hugo Alvar Henrik Aalto. The other direction that emerged focused on the interpretation and reconstruction of the values, formal language, and spatial types of traditional Chinese architectural culture that were never really lost. Finding an architectural practice that can organically weave these two directions together and create its own unique architectural language and intellectual system is rare.

The practice of Zhu Xiaofeng somehow rises to this occasion, forging ahead on this path. Now, if the rise of modern architecture in China was accompanied by a process of Westernization, then it must be recognized that Liang Sicheng's contemporaries[1] who brought the Western model of modern architecture education to China also delivered a critical sense of heritage toward traditional Chinese architectural forms.

In this book of his practice's selected works, Zhu divides his completed architectural projects over the past near two decades into three categories: Courtyard Settlement, Free Cell, and Extension of Home. This division is not so much based on architectural forms, but is rather a reflection of his design strategy.

First and foremost, Zhu's design strategy shows both a respect for and active use of a site's scenery. The English word "scenic" not only refers to natural beauty, but also hints at themes like landscape and drama. Incorporating the word "scenic" as part of his studio's name, Zhu reveals his ongoing contemplation of, and dedication to scenery. "Scenic" encompasses both natural and artificial landscapes, but more importantly, it insinuates the relationship between tradition and modernity.

In terms of spatial organization, material selection, color configuration, and construction methods, Zhu tries to combine local culture with contemporary design language. In his works, Zhu often presents familiar elements like courtyards, traditional gable roofs, and white walls with dark tiles, often in an unconventional way, expressing a kind of inversion and transition between the known and unknown, and between regular and irregular. He thus reinterprets the understanding of scenery, achieves in creating it, and consequently pens the dialogue between tradition and modernity.

After completing his undergraduate studies at Shenzhen University in southern China, Zhu stayed at the university's design institute for three years and taught design courses. In 1997, he entered Harvard Graduate School of Design (GSD), and after graduating in 1999, he spent five years working at KPF in New York. Chinese architecture at the end of the twentieth century was still largely concerned with the study and imitation of Western architecture, and perhaps his studies at Harvard helped him to maintain a certain distance from the Chinese architectural trends of that time and become more aware of the value of Chinese architectural culture. Just like I.M. Pei's graduation design at GSD—a traditional Chinese courtyard design for an art museum in Shanghai—these early thoughts on Chinese tradition did not materialize until many years later. Although, it was in Zhu's early practice in the Qingpu and Jiading suburbs of Shanghai, where he developed his style after returning to China, that he truly began tying his practice to the spatial typology and cultural temperament of traditional Chinese architecture.

I recall, in 2013—when I was curating "Architectural Practices of Qingpu and Jiading" for the Hong Kong Biennale 2013—Shanghai, much like New York, boasted considerable financial resources, but was more interested in the commercial returns on architecture than in encouraging young independent architects to explore original and innovative projects. Many young studios, including the now famous Atelier Deshaus and Atelier Z+, were not given the opportunity to work in the heart of the city, so instead, they finished a series of projects in the remote suburbs of Qingpu and Jiading, free from administrative interference and constraints. These works allowed them to rise to prominence and gain interest through national and international exhibitions and media coverage. It was during this period that the beautiful landscape of China's Jiangnan region, located just south of the Yangtze River, and its vernacular architecture characterized by whitewashed courtyards left their mark on Zhu's practice. During this period, he expressed the tradition of Chinese architecture through the vernacular characteristics of the Jiangnan region, or the style called "New Jiangnan Water Town."

In Shengli Street Neighborhood Committee and Senior Citizens' Daycare Center, a traditional timber frame system serves as the basic organizational principle for the buildings. The system of wooden beams and purlins largely transcribes and modernizes a traditional structure, while the colors used in the building blend completely into the surrounding historical environment. Two other works of that period—Community Pavilion at Jintao Village and Zhujiajiao Museum of Humanities and Arts—also exhibit characteristics of traditional Chinese architectural elements: sloping roofs, white walls, and wooden wall insertions, yet the integration of a modern architectural language distinguishes these projects from a traditional architectural style. Zhujiajiao Museum of Humanities and Arts merges the white and abstract modernist vocabulary with the white walls and gray tiles of Jiangnan dwellings and enhances the building interface made of brick walls and wooden doors and windows to the scale of the entire façade. The two buildings show typological characteristics of two types of contemporary architecture. Firstly, both structures are public buildings visibly located in the center of a square or open space, which differentiates them from traditional Jiangnan dwellings that are embedded and hidden in the urban or village texture of their surroundings—therefore, all façades of the buildings needed to be carefully designed. Second, the resulting contemporary interpretation of the courtyard no longer locks-in the courtyard within peripheral buildings, rather, the courtyard becomes an interlocutor for the integration with the urban space.

The interest in polygons, bifurcations, and honeycomb shapes that was first apparent in Community Pavilion at Jintao Village has since culminated in two other projects: Shanghai Google Creators' Society Center and Bilingual Kindergarten Affiliated to East China Normal University. These two buildings typologically correspond to the figure-ground relationship of hexagons. The Google center forms elongated volumes intersecting the environment and trees in mid-air, aiming to dissipate its own mass and to achieve a sense of emptiness. The reflective mirrored walls on the ground level reinforce the ambiguity of the building, creating a second floor that seemingly floats, and the twisted metal strips of the façade further deconstruct the building's volume into a two-dimensional woven plane. On the other hand, the kindergarten is the exact opposite, displaying a repeating superposition and combination of hexagonal honeycomb-like units with bright white walls and overlapping wooden surfaces. An interesting difference between the projects is the design of the pathways. In the Y-shaped structure of the Google center, the walkways are minimal in size, while the walkways along the outside of the kindergarten's hexagonal courtyards are much larger, which fits to the spatial appeal and recreational needs of the kindergarten.

Zhu uses the same modular structure in Bridge of Nine Terraces, which he designed for the 11th Jiangsu Horticultural Exposition. The bridge consists of nine 13-by-26-feet (4-by-8-meter) platforms that take on the shape of nine progressively ascending and descending cabin rooms. The employed strategies toward the building's structure and the combination of modules elegantly respond to the complex requirements of the bridge in terms of span, height, and forms of use. Together, they paint a graceful and spacious curve across the water. The nine platforms are suspended from arched, folded plate trusses that are hidden inside the sloping roof of the bridge. In this design, the traditional bridge of Jiangnan water towns is creatively reborn through a contemporary structural and architectural language, which also highlights the bridge's role as a public space for the village, as well as a symbol of homecoming.

Departing from sites that connect to the larger fabric of the townscape or cityscape, Deep Dive Rowing Club in Shanghai's Century Park and Lattice Book House on the West Bund in Shanghai are located on standalone plots. The rowing club attaches to the waterside, with its horizontal space covered by a pitched roof with a central skylight, showcasing windowsill benches completely open to the river. This design establishes a link to traditional Chinese waterside pavilions, while simultaneously keeping a distance from them, offering a contemporary approach to this spatial prototype and its details. Similarly, Lattice Book House on the West Bund extends the spatial logic of the spiraling space of a similar design not featured in this collection: Green Valley Art Center. The thin horizontal floor slabs hang within the transparent volume, while the lattice-work structure becomes the dominant theme of the space.

The elongated continuous spaces that Zhu started to explore in Deep Dive Rowing Club became a recurring theme in a series of later works. Activity Homes at Yunjin Road combines those elongated continuous spaces with a simple fluctuating pitched-roof structure to create a series of public spaces that open up along the side. Dongyuan Qianxun Community Center in Suzhou is a good representation of Scenic Architecture Office's current focus on the combination of modern architectural concepts such as structure, space, and materials, with landscapes and garden spaces that are characteristic of the Jiangnan region. Here, the archetypal continuous space covered by an inverted concrete barrel roof and the spatial sequence of traditional gardens are superimposed to create a strangely familiar feeling. On the one hand, the stacked walls and the inverted barrel roof structure correspond well with the functional layout of the building, expressing the architect's exploration of the importance of structure in architecture. On the other hand, the abstract garden with its scraggy landscape scene, neat and calm water surfaces, and changes of light and shade within the courtyards showcase the Jiangnan flair.

Zhu's two largest works carry on his persistent focus on the combination of linear spaces, the advancement of the courtyard series, and the staggered composition of large and small rooftops. Dashawan Beach Facility at Lianyungang is a landmark seaside building with a strong sense of composition and a touch of mega-architecture, where the stacked linear volumes and the rhythmic motion of the waves create an intrinsic synergy that perfectly echoes the environment. Pudong Adolescent Activity Center and Civic Art Center resembles a miniature city, with building volumes of different scales staggered on platforms of various heights. A few small buildings with double-pitch roofs are scattered on the platforms, sometimes surmounted by larger eaves, thus creating a kind of floating street scenery.

Although these two large-scale projects have their own complexities, they are in fact related to Zhu's long-term contribution to the value discourse of Chinese architecture. On the surface, double-pitch roofs, courtyards, and structural systems of beams and columns are just architectural elements or fragments, but if we compare his work with the research of European architects on Oriental architecture—like that of Jørn Utzon—we can discover the profound thinking behind Zhu's works—namely that architecture and its forms are, in fact, extensions of human beings. In his doctoral dissertation, Zhu describes architecture as an extension of human beings.[2] Further, through his study of the relationship between primitive architecture and the human body, and his research on the practice of Taiwanese architect Chen Chi-kwan[3] on a campus of Tunghai University, he extends the existing ontological perspective of architecture by assuming a more macroscopic perspective of it as a "human extension," exploring it in terms of "body–mind, ontology, and interaction."

As architecture breaks from the mechanized reproduction of traditional construction methods according to the textbook, the architect's critical mind, as the main subject of design, begins to emerge. In that vein, the Western understanding of the essence of space—for human use—becomes the scale for architects to reflexively observe or measure design and construction.

The rapid advancement of contemporary Chinese architecture was accompanied by leaps in architectural scale. In this almost frenzied pursuit of "bigness," the human body as a scale of reference got lost and became nowhere to be found. Today, these "empty" buildings, with floor areas of tens of thousands of square meters, that create the myth of rapid construction, have become the physical manifestation of our time. In Zhu's works, he echoes the casualness of the body and uses this strategy to create a spatial scale that is connected to humans. This is also a conscious resistance to the myth of "bigness" permeating through contemporary China.

In this sense, the significance of Zhu's architecture moves away from the simple imitation and reproduction of traditional architectural forms toward a kind of architecture similar to the concept of "embodiment" in Western architectural theory. In fact, the palaces in the East adopt a scale that is closer to the human body than the grand and lofty palaces in the West. In the Forbidden City in Beijing, we can observe that even the central buildings, such as the Three Great Halls, are relatively consistent and in line with the human scale, while the grandeur of the entire Forbidden City is organized in hundreds of smaller buildings through multiple courtyards and corridors. In Zhu's works, we can see that he consciously or unconsciously limits the volume of individual spaces to two floors, which draws close to the scale of the human body, while courtyards and corridors become the internal logic for organizing spatial sequences. In this aspect, his works are an apt example of his theory about architecture as an extension of human beings and the human body.

From a passive reproduction of the Jiangnan aesthetic that is adapted to the regional environment, to an "embodied" architecture with a more subjective value assessment, Zhu's work bridges the divide between modernist architectural language and traditional Chinese architectural forms. Through that, he makes an important contribution to contemporary Chinese architectural culture; or rather, to a new tradition of architecture.

1. Liang Sicheng (梁思成 ; 1901–1972), was a Chinese architecture historian, architect, urban planner, and educator. He worked with the China Construction Society, the first academic organization devoted to the study of traditional architecture. In 1946, he set up the Department of Architecture in Tsinghua University, where he served as professor and dean of the department until his death.

2. Zhu Xiaofeng, "Architecture as Extension of Human: Studies on Three Fundamental Paths of Architectural Evolution," PhD dissertation (Shanghai: Tongji University, 2000).

3. Chen Chi-kwan (陈其宽 ; 1921–2007), was an architect, urban planner, painter, and educator. He was the founder of the Department of Architecture at Tunghai University.

Zhu Xiaofeng

Founding Principal, Scenic Architecture Office
Guest Professor, College of Architecture and Urban Planning,
Tongji University
Chartered Member, RIBA
Member, Architectural Culture Academic Committee of Chinese
Architectural Society

Translator: Clemens Ruben

REBIRTH OF FORM-TYPE

The beginning of the twenty-first century was an era of uncertainty. Today, environmental crises, technology explosions, and conflicts such as "globalization versus geostrategy" take center stage as the main topics of contemporary civilization. A revolution has hit many physical and artificial virtual systems, and architecture is no exception. Having come into being in as early as the primitive age, architecture is one of the oldest extensions of existence, just like clothes, pottery, and self-fashioned tools. However, then, it had to respond only to nature, body–mind, family, and tribe. In today's modern world, architecture has to respond to needs far beyond those basics. Over its thousands of years of development, architecture has evolved significantly by accumulating its own rules and aligning itself with the impetus of external forces. In that time, it has also undertaken many sophisticated pursuits in order to conform to the influences of economy, politics, culture, technology, and media.

The modernist architecture movement started (somewhat belatedly) 130 years after the Industrial Revolution. In comparison, contemporary architecture responds much faster to the times, especially when it comes to technology, even appearing to possess extra "lift" with proper media packaging. However, despite their variances, the themes behind external appearances have never changed, and therein lies the conflict between the inherent inertia of architecture and the external forces that influence it. In today's world, the original connection between architecture and body–mind is fast disappearing; the cultural attributes of architectural ontology have been weakened and the architectural practice has been constrained by the value of efficiency. To some extent, contemporary architecture—in keeping pace with the times like other artificial systems—has also been coerced by technological rationalism, and has sunk into a new crisis.

In 2004, I founded the practice of Scenic Architecture Office in Shanghai with the original intention to explore architecture that merges traditional and contemporary culture in the southeast Yangtze River Delta region where I grew up. As the years passed running my practice, and the world changed, I began to think about the essence behind my original intention and our attitudes toward the era's revolution, and I tried to combine these two aspects to renew the direction of our practice.

It was 2,500 years ago that the ancient Chinese philosopher Laozi had revealed in *Tao Te Ching*, the yin (void) and yang (entity) of architectural noumenon and presented the relevance between substance, space, and human. Later, in the mid-nineteenth century, Gottfried Semper summarized architecture as four elements and established the anthropology-oriented tectonic theory. These philosophies and theories in architecture's origins strengthened my understanding of architecture as an extension of human beings. Thus, I regard the evolution of architecture to be the result of the co-action between body–mind, ontology, and interaction.

Body–mind is the starting point of all synthetic creations and almost every action of construction is born from the needs of body–mind. From individuals to families to social groups, body–mind is the entity that experiences and uses architecture at its most basic level; answering to the needs of body–mind, people create architecture. Architecture ontology reflects the autonomy of architecture, which has its own rules of space and time, tectonics, typology, and so on. Interaction refers to the mutual impact between architecture, the natural environment, and other artificial extensions, including culture, technology, politics, economy, and so on. Interaction pushes or constrains the development of architecture from the outside. For architecture to successfully evolve, it must consider and contemplate the basic point of body–mind, the inner core of ontology, and the interaction of external forces. Having their own mechanisms, these three co-acting aspects have played different roles through the different eras to propel the evolution of architecture. I refer to this attitude and method of observing architecture as "a perspective of extension," which, I believe, can help us to thoroughly understand the history of architecture, and to rationally evaluate the crisis and opportunities of modern times.

In my practice, I have been consciously connecting the past, touching the present, and exploring the future through these three aspects. On the body–mind level, we explore new settlement models based on individual experiences and the collective needs of contemporary society. On the ontological level, we pursue the unity of substance and space–time by combining tectonic and space as mutual complements. On the interaction level, we place nature and technology at an equal level and try to realize their fusion, rather than instigate a conflict

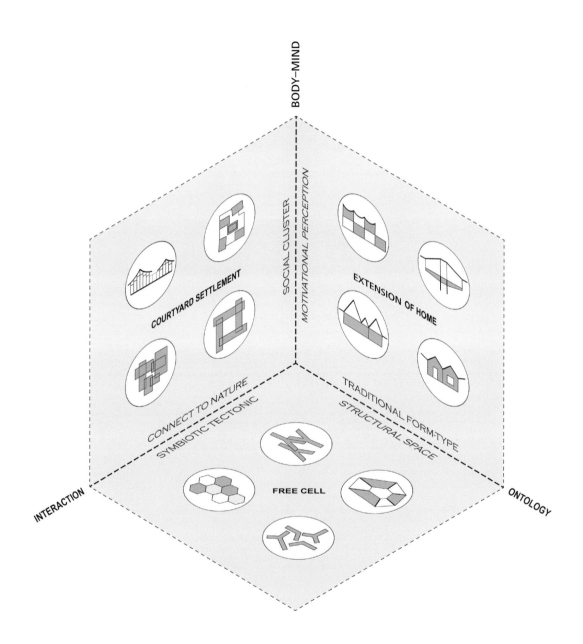

between the two. And the key to enabling and actualizing these three aspects is "form-type." This word, or concept, if you will, is something I created to refer to a form-oriented architectural typology based on tectonic and spatial forms, which holds intrinsic and active links with people, settlement, nature, culture, technology, and society. Scenic Architecture Office firmly believes in the value of form-type in cultural inheritance and development, and so we explore the regeneration of form-type in each of our projects.

In this first monograph, we showcase twelve works divided into three categories: Courtyard Settlement, Free Cell, and Extension of Home. Courtyard Settlement highlights the reconstruction of the spatial form-type of the courtyard; Free Cell features experiments of new form-types; and Extension of Home takes a look at the expansion of a traditional house form-type. Through explorations of form-type, we aim to bridge the past, present, and future with architecture, and enable it as a conduit for cultural memory, the era's energy, and a balanced and dynamic connection between human, nature, and society.

Human beings who extend architecture with form are unconsciously shaped by architecture. Let us bestow upon architecture kindness and wisdom, for the sake of our civilization and the nature this civilization inhabits.

People surround courtyards with buildings

As an extension of body and mind, beyond the home

A courtyard is a tranquil place

It sparks interaction between people and nature

It encourages human communication

Courtyards embody the idea of the unity between humanity and heaven

We adopt the spatial form of the courtyard as our core

Organizing functions, encapsulating technology, and embracing nature

To explore the future of courtyards

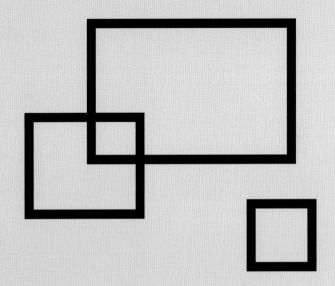

COURTYARD SETTLEMENT

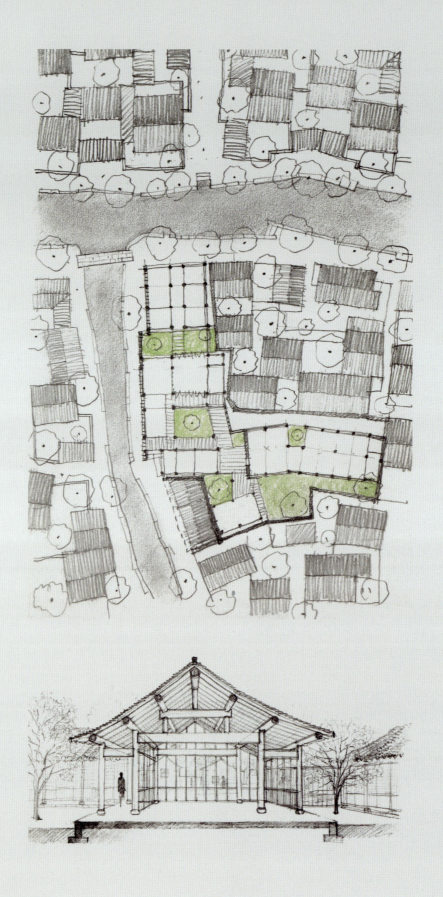

Shengli Street Neighborhood Committee and Senior Citizens' Daycare Center

Reviving Courtyards in a Historic Neighborhood

Location | Zhujiajiao Town, Qingpu District, Shanghai, China
Program | Neighborhood committee and senior citizens' daycare center, and community services
Site area | 7,136.5 ft² (663 m²)
Gross floor area | 5,403.5 ft² (502 m²)
Designed/built | 2007/2011
Design team | Zhu Xiaofeng, Xu Lei, Ding Xufen, Dong Zhiping
Client | Zhujiajiao Town Government
Local design institute | Shanghai Archin (International) Design Consultants Pte Ltd
Structural system | Wooden structure characteristics of traditional constructions in southeast Yangtze River Delta
Main materials | Cinereous brick pavement, Chinese-tile roof, wood partition, and wood-framed door and window

With authentically preserved streetscapes, old bridges, and courtyard architectures from the Ming and Qing dynasties, Zhujiajiao, also known as the Venice of Shanghai, attracts an increasing number of visitors every year.

Shengli Street, home to many of the town's elderly inhabitants, is a quiet neighborhood located at the southeast corner of Zhujiajiao, far from the crowded northern tourist area. The new Neighborhood Committee and Senior Citizens' Daycare Center sits at an intersection of two small rivers and provides community services for the locals.

As the site is situated within the historical preservation district, the urban planning bureau requested that the new building respect and follow its traditional surroundings in terms of scale and architectural style. Therefore, we used the traditional timber structure and tectonic system as our basic architectural language to structure a cluster of buildings along five dispersed courtyards, based on the center's program and circulation. These semi-public courtyards of various sizes, designed as scattered venues within the settlement, are interconnected to the site's old-town structures. We delighted in weaving the spatial configuration such that it plays with the light and shadows in the courtyards, amiably conversing with its historic surroundings.

The design of the center is traditional, obligingly blending in with its older neighbors, except for a wood-framed curtain wall that faces the river. We conceptualized this variance to emphasize the building as a public facility instead of a private residence, and to, in a way, inform the community of the center's presence and availability. As architects, we enjoyed this design process and saw no need to further pursue any other distinguishing forms.

A unitary form-type does not hinder the freedom of space in modality and spirit. Hence, why worry about the form if a void is just as inspiring and refreshing to behold?

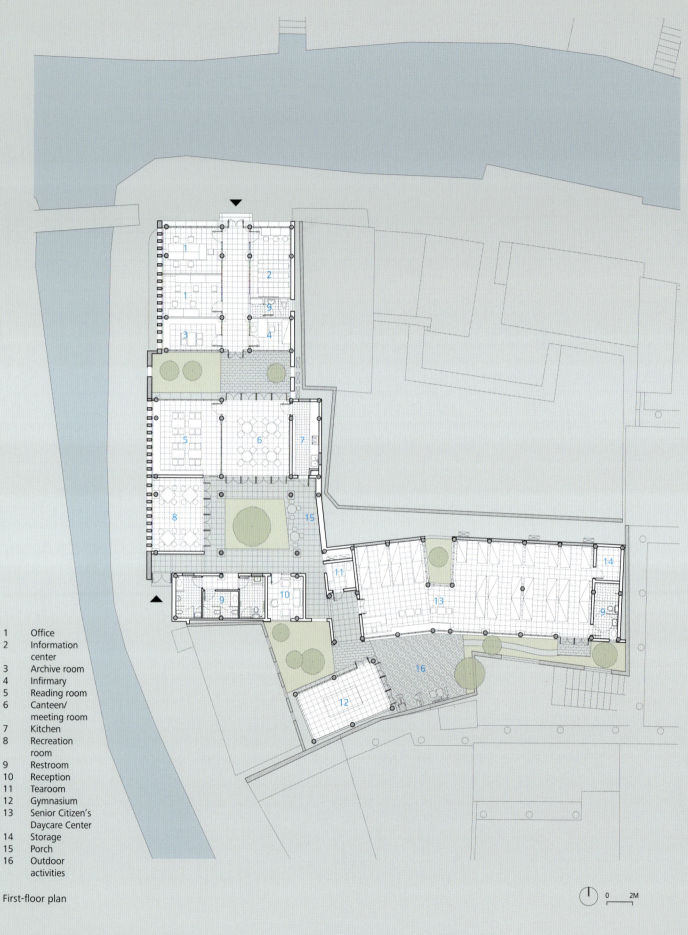

1 Office
2 Information center
3 Archive room
4 Infirmary
5 Reading room
6 Canteen/ meeting room
7 Kitchen
8 Recreation room
9 Restroom
10 Reception
11 Tearoom
12 Gymnasium
13 Senior Citizen's Daycare Center
14 Storage
15 Porch
16 Outdoor activities

First-floor plan

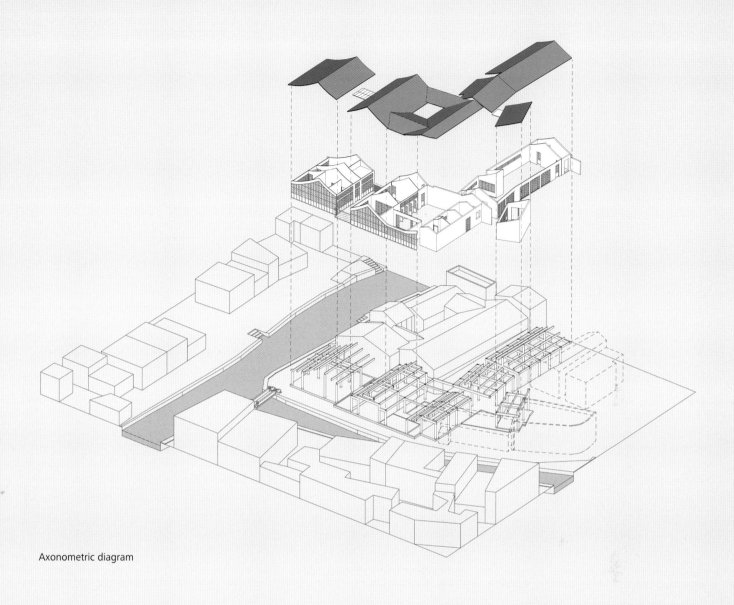
Axonometric diagram

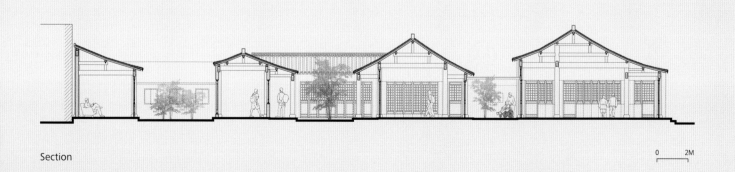
Section

0 2M

1 Traditional-style small blue-black tile
40 mm straw mat
Non-woven fabric barrier
35 mm foam glass insulation board
1.2 mm polyurethane waterproof layer
210x120x20 mm traditional-style shedthins tile
Timber rafter @240 mm

2 300x300x35 mm cinereous brick pavement
1:3 20 mm polymer cement mortar binder, topped with cement flour
Cement paste (mixed with construction adhesive)
60 mm C15 concrete subbase
Packed soil
Reinforced-concrete foundation

A renewal of traditional tectonics

The rules in *Law and Origin of Tectonics*, an ancient Chinese classic on timber structure systems in southern Yangtze River Delta, highlights the traditional post-and-lintel and column-and-tie systems. These systems help save materials and enable the design of flexible spaces that can evolve further, if so needed. In aligning with architectural tectonics, the traditional waterproofing and insulation system is improved with contemporary technology.

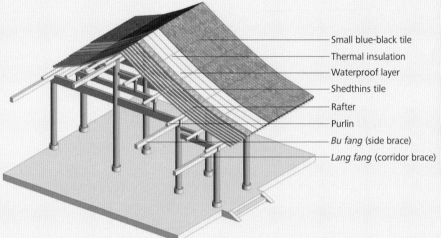

- Small blue-black tile
- Thermal insulation
- Waterproof layer
- Shedthins tile
- Rafter
- Purlin
- *Bu fang* (side brace)
- *Lang fang* (corridor brace)

Facing the river, the west gable flaunts a wood-framed curtain wall with big windows, emphasizing the building as a public facility. The windows allow people who pass by to catch a glimpse of the activities taking place within, inviting the curious to step into the center for a closer look. These thoughtfully composed architectural and design details translate as familiar forms that keep alive the memory of the residences in the area, while presenting new ideas to the neighborhood.

A unitary form-type will not hinder the freedom of space in modality and spirit. Why worry about the form if the void can equally inspire fresh perspectives?

We enjoyed weaving the spatial configuration such that it played with the light and shadows in the courtyards, while also respecting its historical surroundings.

Zhujiajiao Museum of Humanities and Arts

Convergence of Frames

Location | Zhujiajiao Town, Qingpu District, Shanghai, China
Program | Fine art museum and exhibition
Site area | 15,586 ft² (1,448 m²)
Gross floor area | 19,569 ft² (1,818 m²)
Designed/built | 2008/2010
Design team | Zhu Xiaofeng, Xu Lei, Li Qitong, Dong Zhiping, Zhang Hao
Client | Shanghai Dianshanhu New Town Development Co. Ltd
Local design institute | Shanghai Xiandai Huagai Architectural Design Co. Ltd
Structural system | Reinforced-concrete and steel framework
Main materials | Painted white walls, insulated thermal glass, zinc-panel roofing, and local granite

Zhujiajiao is a well-preserved water town in Shanghai with a history of more than 1,700 years. The site, located at the entrance of the old town, faces two 480-year-old ginkgo trees. The museum houses paintings and artworks related to the history of Zhujiajiao. The museum's design strives to offer an art-appreciation experience that we hope will become deeply rooted in the culture of Zhujiajiao as time passes; the anchored architecture of the museum helps materialize and shape this experience.

At the heart of the configuration is the central atrium. Encircled by white walls, it resembles a covered courtyard that basks under a dazzling skylight. Arranged around this atrium, on the first floor, is a series of galleries, which escort visitors to a folded staircase that ascends to several dispersed "small-house" galleries on the second floor. These galleries are linked by a corridor that wraps around the atrium.

On the second floor, different types of open courtyards that overlook quaint alleyways and shops weave the surrounding sceneries into the experience of the museum, and let visitors immerse in the nostalgic atmosphere of old-town Zhujiajiao. These courtyards also present diverse spaces to conduct various activities and events. The interspersed gallery–courtyard layout references the figure-ground texture of the old town, and along that concept, orientates visitors such that they meander between artworks and real sceneries.

In the east courtyard, a shallow water pool embraces the reflection of one of the ginkgo trees, framing it in aqueous mirror that adds an organic drift to the museum's design motion. The gallery spaces are illuminated with a combination of artificial and natural light. Translucent windows cleverly utilize the space between the concrete frameworks and the roof's steel structure, ushering soft daylight into the galleries on the second floor.

As a convergence of frames that defines spaces, collects sceneries, and presents artworks, the museum offers intimate interactions between object and subject.

Master plan

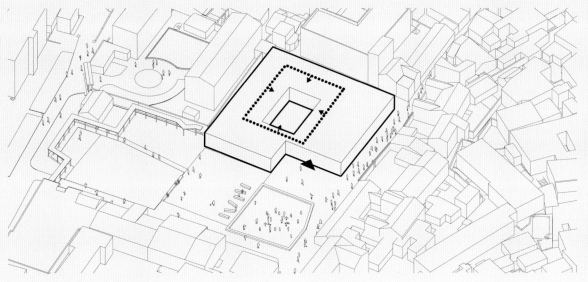
Diagram of integral ground level

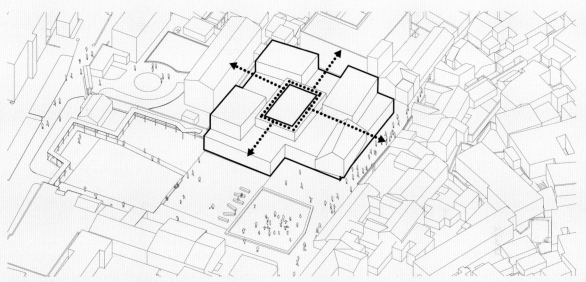
Diagram of dispersed units at second level

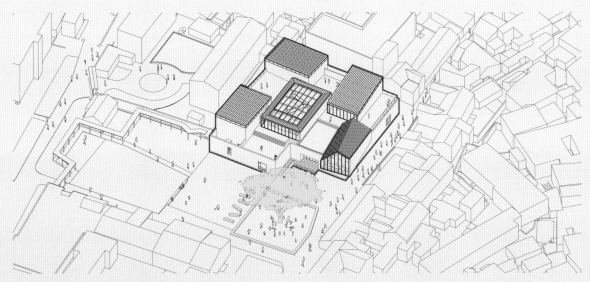
Figure-ground analysis of building and courtyard

045

Second-floor plan

First-floor plan

046

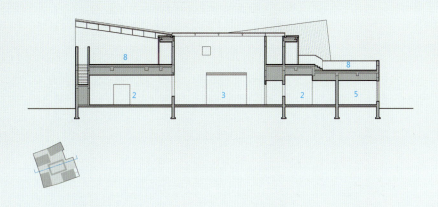

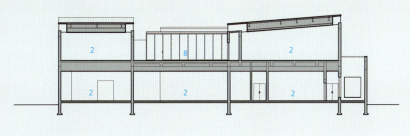

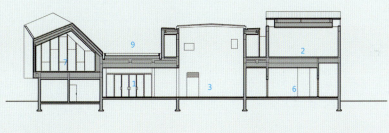

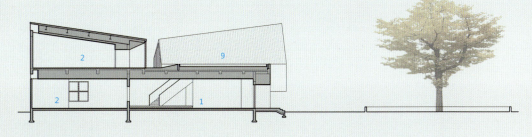

1	Lobby
2	Exhibition hall
3	Atrium
4	Locker room
5	Office
6	Equipment room
7	Café
8	Courtyard
9	Water courtyard

Section

0   5M

047

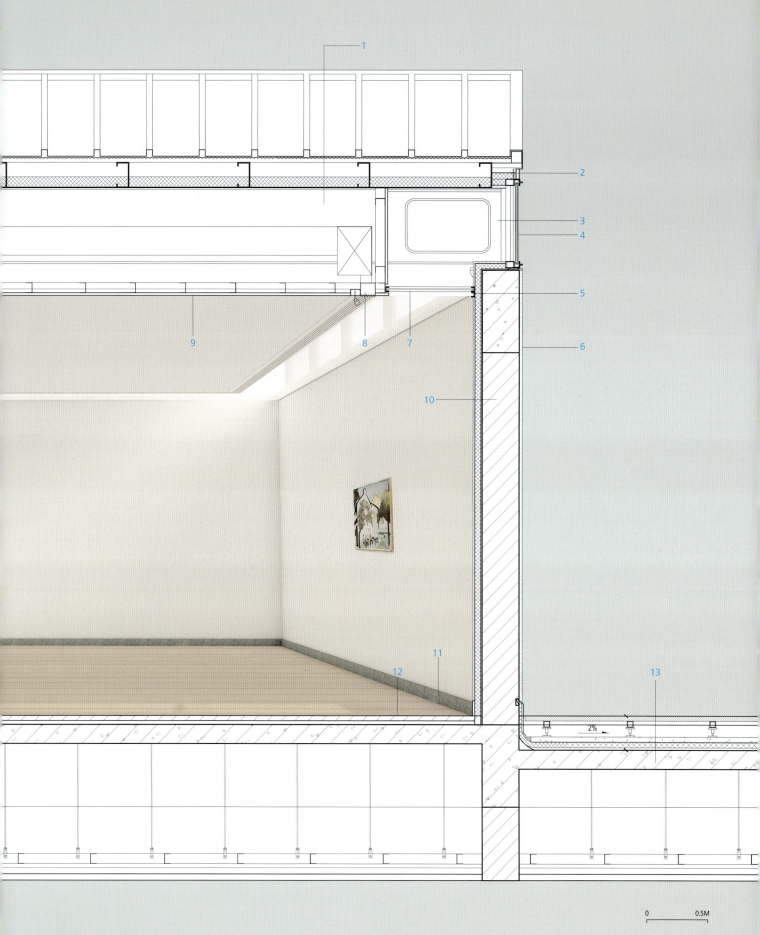

Natural lighting under floating roof

The steel beams supporting the roofs of the second-floor galleries are secured on concrete ring beams. This creates space to install high windows and also lifts the roofs up to create the impression that they are floating.

1	0.7 mm titanium-zinc panel roof 6 mm ventilation and noise reduction mesh 3 mm waterproof membrane 0.8 mm galvanized steel plate leveling blanket 0.5 mm profiled steel sheet 40 mm XPS insulation with steel mesh 160×85×10 mm steel purlin Steel beam
2	Aluminum channel bar
3	Hole at the end of steel beam
4	Insulated frosted glass
5	Metal slot for hanging art
6	Sand-gel paint for exterior wall
7	Translucent membrane
8	Air-conditioning vent
9	White latex paint Paper-surface gypsum board ceiling
10	White latex paint 9 mm gypsum board Blockboard base 60 mm light steel keel 30 mm XPS insulated layer Concrete hollow-block wall
11	Brushed, stainless-steel baseboard
12	Composite oak flooring
13	Anticorrosive timber flooring Raised floor space 40 mm concrete Non-woven fabric barrier 35 mm PUF insulated layer 1.5 mm non-tar-based polyurethane waterproof coating Lightweight concrete sloping Cast-in-place reinforced-concrete roof slab

To introduce natural light evenly into the interior spaces, rectangular holes were carved out at both ends of the beams.

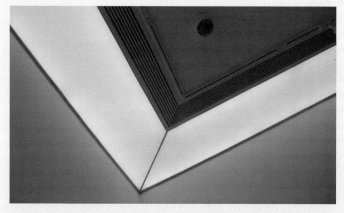

Natural light enters through the translucent glass windows and filters in through the PTFE membranes alongside the ceilings. The morphing reflections and refractions scatter soft daylight throughout and light up the area. Combined with supplementary artificial lighting, a conducive exhibition space with comfortable lighting is created.

Through an anchored architecture that awes and inspires, we aim to shape an experience of art-appreciation, which we hope will find deep roots in Zhujiajiao's culture in time to come.

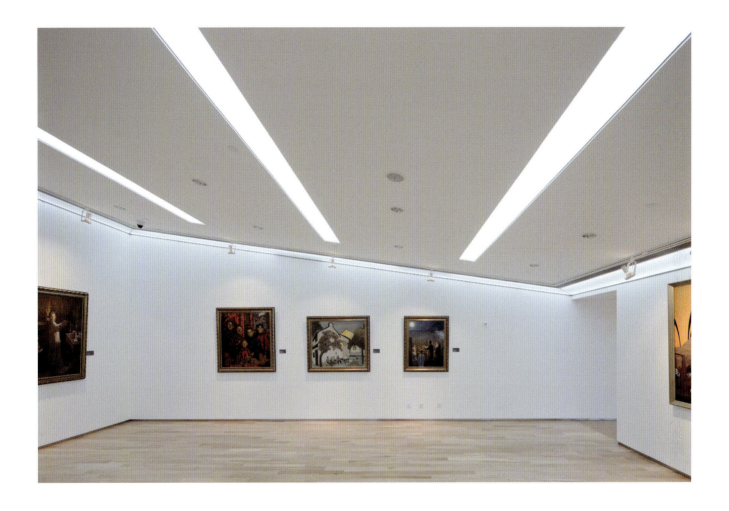

As a convergence of frames that define spaces, collect sceneries, and present paintings, the museum offers an experience of intimate interactions between object and subject.

The two ginkgo trees were originally planted in the backyard of a temple and have been here for 480 years. We hope the museum will prove a worthy companion to the trees as it beholds the future, to witness the next century with them.

Lattice Book House

A Tree of Terraces

Location | Riverfront Park, Xuhui District, Shanghai, China
Program | Retail (book store and café)
Gross floor area | 3,767 ft² (350 m²)
Designed/built | 2014/2016
Design team | Zhu Xiaofeng, Li Qitong (project manager), Liang Shan (project architect), Zhang Pingting
Client | Xuhui Riverfront Development Investment and Construction Ltd
Local design institute | Tongji University Institute of Architectural Design and Research
Structural system | Steel lattice walls and steel grid beams
Main materials | Dark-gray fluorocarbon paint, laminated bamboo floor and ceiling, aluminum profile with internal angle steel, low-iron laminated thermal low-E glass, stainless-steel handrail, and cement fiberboard

Embraced by a thick grove that is part of the broad scenery along Huangpu River, Lattice Book House is a book café located in the Xuhui Riverfront Park on the West Bund of Shanghai. Lattice Book House, designed as a group of terraces, has been constructed to merge into its natural setting to provide citizens with cozy spaces for recreation and communication.

Passing along either the riverside path or the flower alley—renovated from the old railway—one will come upon an intriguing sprawl of wooden terraces "floating" in the grove. Supported by steel lattice walls, these terraces of different heights are connected by stairs that artfully zigzag between them. Following the trail of stairs, visitors will discover a cluster of interrelated spaces that open out to each other. The combination of lattice walls with transparent glass walls blurs confined boundaries and transforms this stack of terraces into a fluid blend of interior and exterior spaces. The scenic backdrop of the grove greets every corner of the building, making it a real treat to idle the hours away browsing the many books displayed on the lattice-wall bookshelves. The compelling ambiance continuously fuses sensory indulgence and imagery to create captivating experiences beyond the thrill of a good book.

Composed of C-channel steel and steel panels, the supporting bookshelf structure defines, as well as guides, the formation and use of the spaces. Main ducts reach each terrace along the main, arterial stairs, which mimics a tree trunk conveying nutrition to branches and leaves. Beams, drainage, and other building mechanics are hidden within the 17.7-inch-high (450-millimeter-high) platforms, enabling a seamless integration of function, mechanical systems, and structure.

By ingeniously blending structure, furnishings, and space, this building becomes a physical medium that establishes a positive relationship between scale, space, and perception—the very origin of architectural spirit.

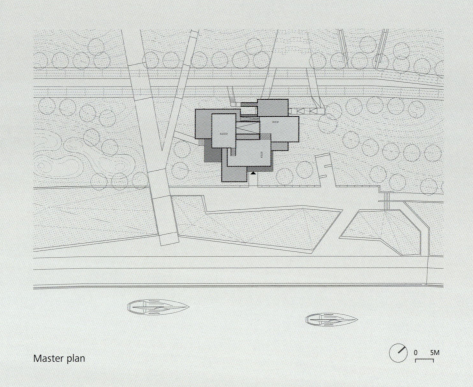

Master plan

0 5M

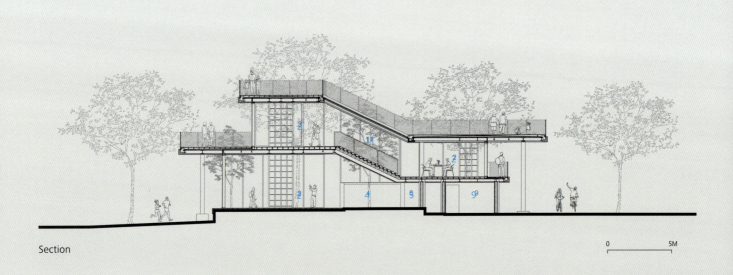

Section

0 5M

1	Lobby	7	Equipment platform
2	Book café	8	Accessible restroom
3	Outdoor platform	9	Men's restroom
4	Service area	10	Ladies' restroom
5	Operations area	11	Grand stairs
6	Storage		

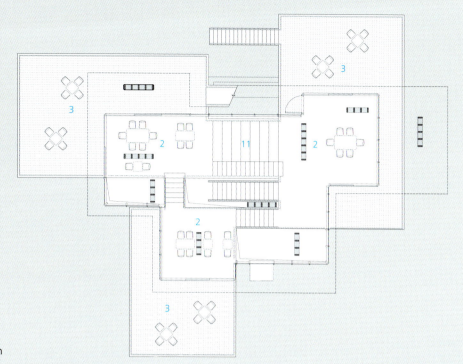

Second-floor plan

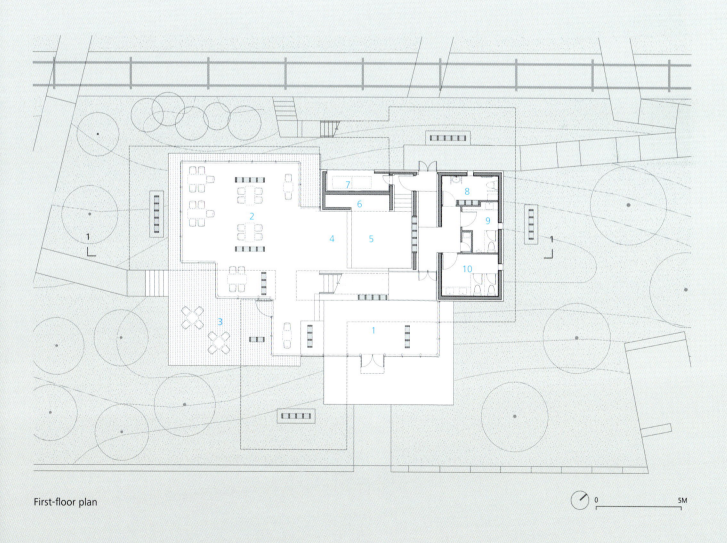

First-floor plan

0   5M

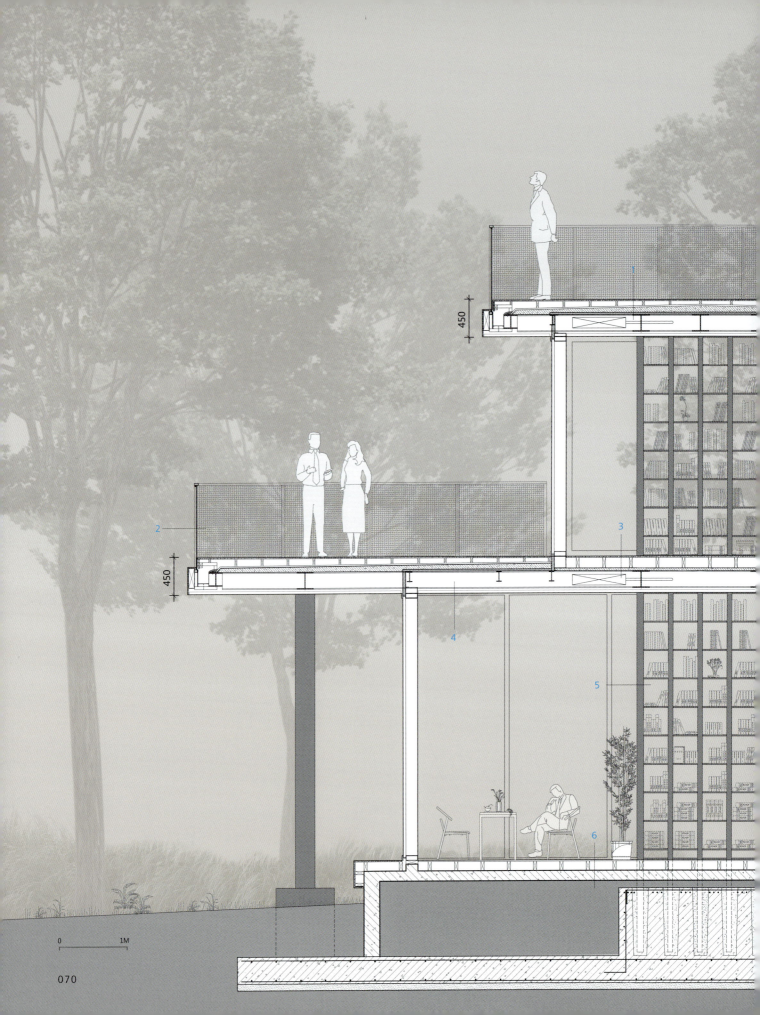

Highly integrated tectonics between structure, space, and MEP

1. 18 mm composite bamboo exterior flooring
   40x60 mm @400 steel tube keel
   20 mm 1:3 cement mortar protection
   3 mm + 3 mm double layer SBS modified asphalt waterproof membrane
   35 mm 1:3 cement mortar sloping
   30 mm RPUF insulation
   4 mm riffled steel plate
   Steel structure

2. 58x50 mm stainless-steel T-shaped stand
   Stainless-steel mesh with 20 mm spacing

3. 14 mm composite bamboo interior flooring
   156 mm timber keel @400
   40 mm fine-aggregate concrete
   Cement mortar binder
   4 mm riffled steel plate
   Steel structure

4. 40x20 mm composite bamboo grating ceiling
   Lightweight steel keel
   Steel structure

5. Polyurethane acrylic paint
   Epoxy-mio barrier paint
   Epoxy-zinc primer paint
   Steel structure

6. 14 mm composite bamboo interior flooring
   135 mm timber keel
   100 mm C15 concrete subbase
   150 mm gravel
   Packed soil

17.7-inch (450-millimeter) platform = structure + drainage + air-conditioning + lighting + floor and ceiling finis

Most MEP ducts are laid along the stairs and reach the terminals through holes on the beams. The drainage, air-conditioning unit, lighting, and floor and ceiling finishes are all integrated in the 17.7-inch-high (450-millimeter-high) platforms.

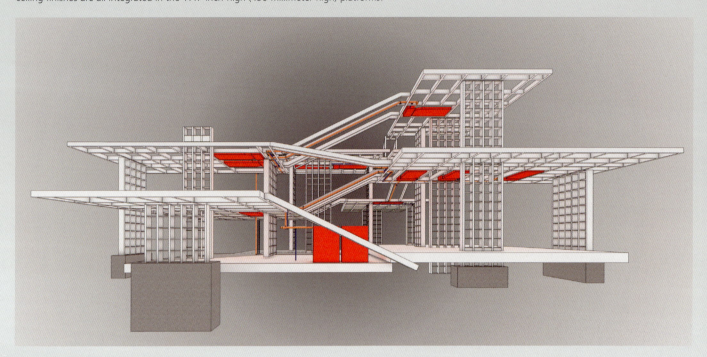

Lattice wall = structure + spatial definition + furniture + cable tube

The steel lattice walls are embedded and cast into the concrete foundation, and two (sometimes three) of them support a steel lattice platform. The lattice walls are welded by vertical channel steels at 11.8 inches (300 millimeters) and vertical steel plates at 15.7 inches (400 millimeters). The lattice walls also serve as shelves for books, to define spaces, and as channels for cables.

Stairs = vertical circulation + structural element + conduit + open auditorium

Linking platforms of different heights, the steel stairs unite them as a whole to deliver horizontal force and resist torque. Main pipes, like condensers and drainpipes, reach each floor alongside the stairs. The top flight was widened to become seats for the open auditorium.

The evolution of curtain wall corner detail

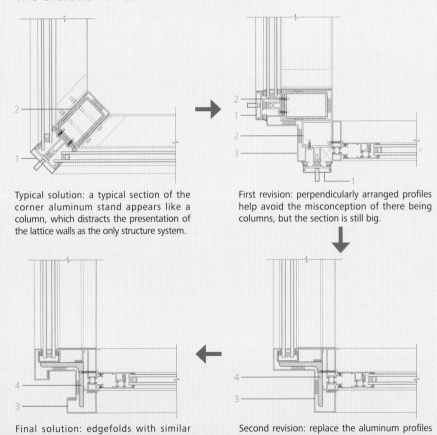

Typical solution: a typical section of the corner aluminum stand appears like a column, which distracts the presentation of the lattice walls as the only structure system.

First revision: perpendicularly arranged profiles help avoid the misconception of there being columns, but the section is still big.

Final solution: edgefolds with similar thickness as the glass create a visual effect of two glazing panels connected with a notch.

Second revision: replace the aluminum profiles with angle steel to reduce the section size.

1	Aluminum cover
2	Aluminum stand
3	1.5 mm aluminum panel
4	Galvanized angle steel

Both books and nature are within reach at every corner of the building.

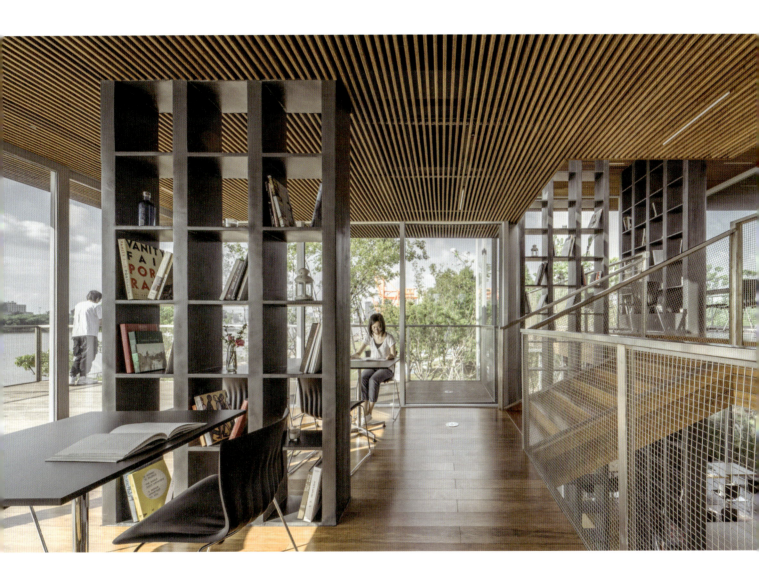

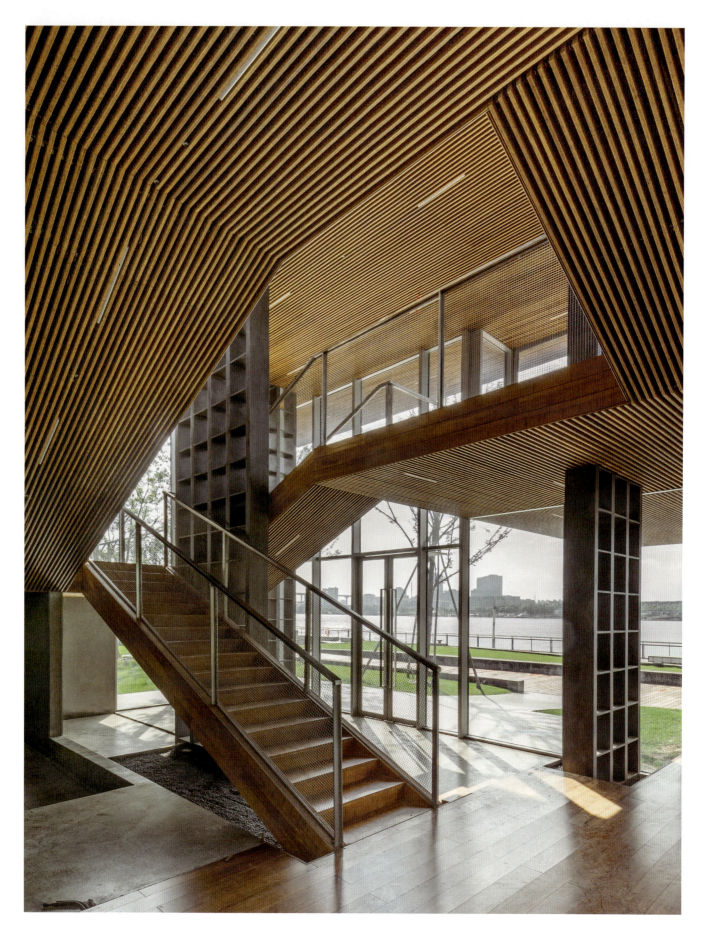

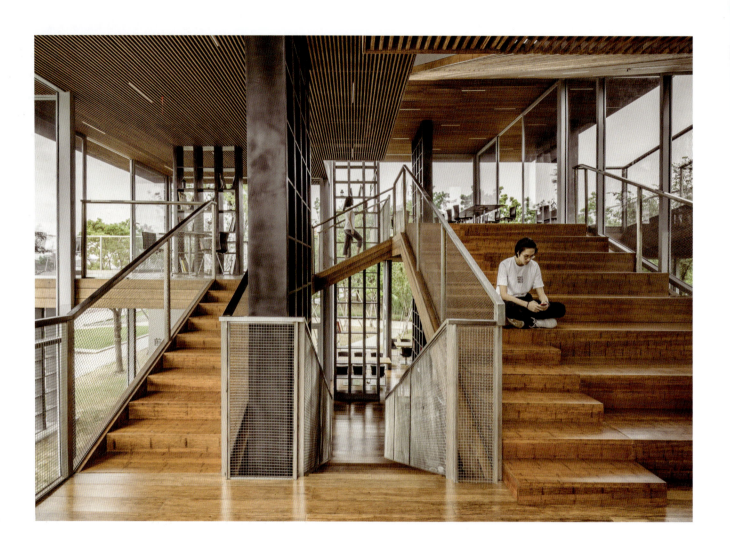

Lattice Book House is a stack of terraces in the grove, fusing sensory indulgence with imagery, for unforgettable moments that extend beyond being engrossed in a good book.

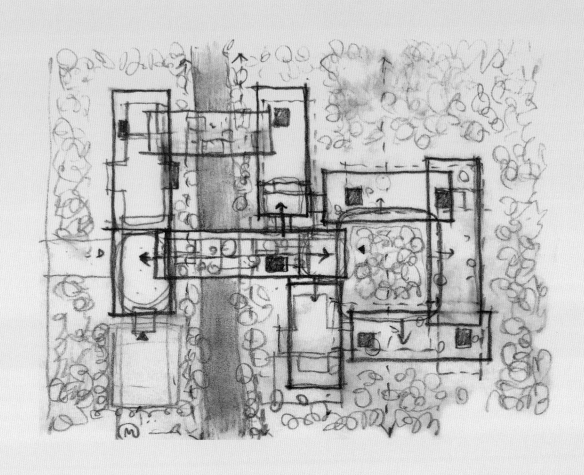
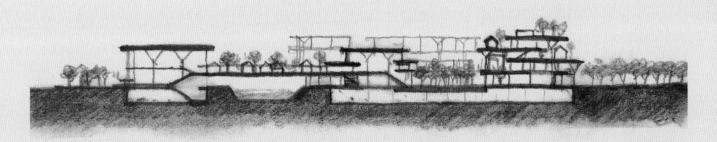

Pudong Adolescent Activity Center and Civic Art Center

Interactive Platforms

Location | Middle Cultural Neighborhood, Pudong New District, Shanghai, China
Program | Auditorium, rehearsal room, exhibition, technology hub, and cultural and arts activities
Site area | 559,153 ft² (51,947 m²)
Gross floor area | 937,633 ft² (87,109 m²)
Designed/built | 2016/2021
Design team | Conceptual and schematic design: Zhu Xiaofeng, Pablo Gonzalez Riera, Zhuang Xinjia, Liang Shan, Du Jie, Sheng Tai, Xi Yu, Shi Yan'an, Zhou Yan, Shen Ziwei, Xie Tao; Design development, construction design, and construction assistance: Zhu Xiaofeng, Zhuang Xinjia, Du Jie, Jiang Meng, Wang Junyuan, Lin Xiaosheng, Hu Xianmei, Gao Min, Gan Yunni, Sha Chengjun, Ye Chenhui, Weng Wenqian, Song Xiaoyue, Sun Haopeng
Client | Shanghai Pudong New District Education Bureau
Local design institute | Tongji Architectural Design (Group) Co. Ltd
Structural system | Steel framework and steel truss
Main materials | Low-iron insulated low-E glass, aluminum panel, cement fiberboard, and perforated aluminum panel

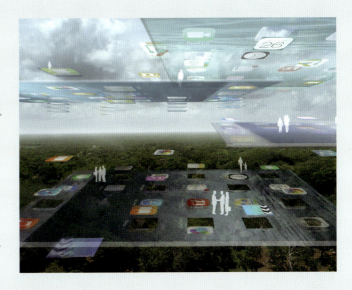

The Pudong Culture Community, planned as a culture hub in Shanghai, will become a new destination for cultural activities in Pudong New District. Located in the middle block of the Culture Community, the site of the Adolescent Activity Center and Civic Art Center is divided by a river into a larger eastern part and a smaller western part. At the northern block of the Culture Community stands the existing Pudong Library (designed by Nihon Sekkei); the Pudong Planning Museum and City Art Center (designed by David Chipperfield Architects) will be built in the southern block. These three blocks will not only be connected below ground, but also be integrated into a common landscape containing other public facilities, such as metro plazas and reading gardens.

To respond to both the outer urban space and the inner functional needs of the project, we designed a multistoried space articulated through interactive platforms. "Boxes" in different scales are scattered on these platforms and house various functions, including, auditoriums, galleries, activity rooms, lobbies, and a cafeteria. The platforms compose the two interlocked courtyard structures. The 1,000-seat auditorium and the Civic Art Center sit on the west courtyard connected to the metro plaza, while the Adolescent Activity Center is located on the east courtyard, which is surrounded by open greenery. By overlapping and linking with each other, the platforms stimulate interactions across the different areas. The garden platform, which spans across the river, links two lobbies on either side and is the spine of public flow. With various indoor/outdoor spaces on the platforms, on the second to the fourth floor, the design frees up ground space, thereby creating an open zone between the library and the Pudong Planning Museum. This forms a pedestrian hub for the entire Culture Community.

The Pudong Culture Community responds to environment and function with a two-pronged concept: the large holistic platforms reciprocate the urban scale, while the "scattered boxes" engage the more intimate scale of individual users. The Adolescent Activity Center and Civic Art Center combines these two scales to not only provide enjoyable spaces for use in the building, but to also convene with the environment in presenting a dynamic public stage for urban life.

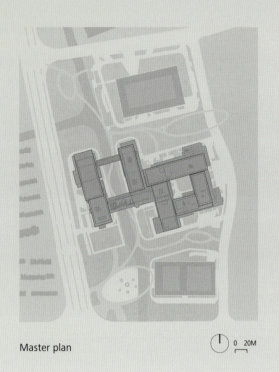

Master plan

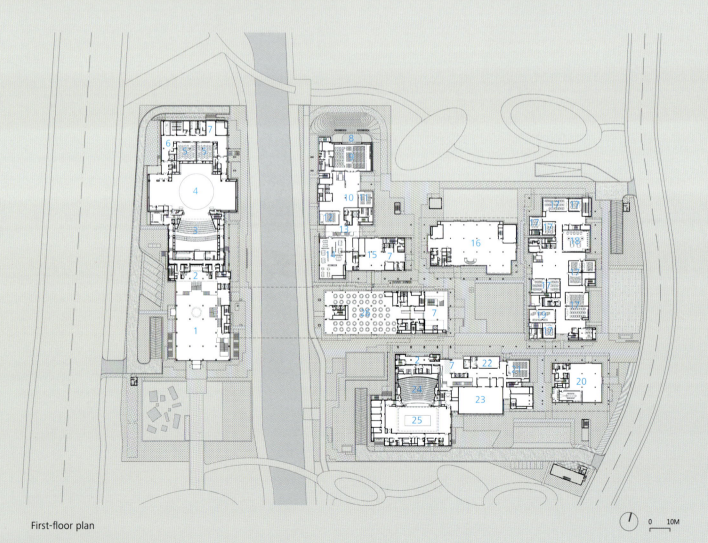

First-floor plan

088

1	West lobby
2	Lounge
3	Auditorium
4	Stage
5	Dressing room
6	Waiting area
7	Foyer
8	Outdoor theater
9	Event theater
10	Digital experience zone
11	Club Room
12	Rehearsal and performance hall
13	Leisure experience area
14	Handcraft workshop (creative space)
15	Exhibition hall
16	Theme activity area
17	Art workshop
18	Pottery workshop
19	Paper art workshop
20	Red Scarf Museum
21	Instrument activity room
22	Recording studio
23	Void leading to lower floor
24	Children's theater auditorium
25	Children's theater stage
26	Restaurant
27	Vestibule
28	Actors' lounge
29	Art classroom
30	Music classroom
31	Model studio
32	Science and technology activity room
33	Dance rehearsal hall
34	Martial arts training hall
35	East lobby
36	Rest pavilion
37	Courtyard

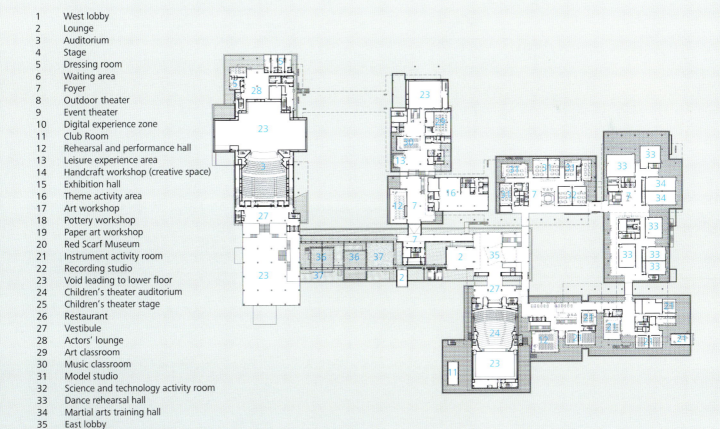

Second-floor plan

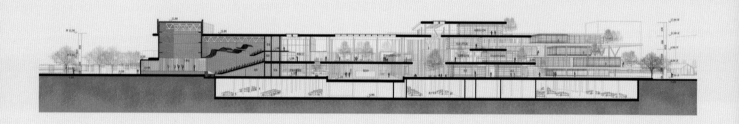
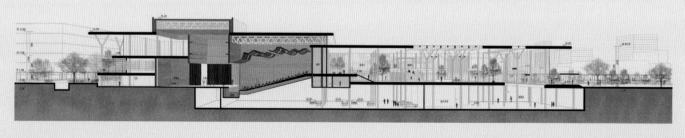

Sections

0 5M

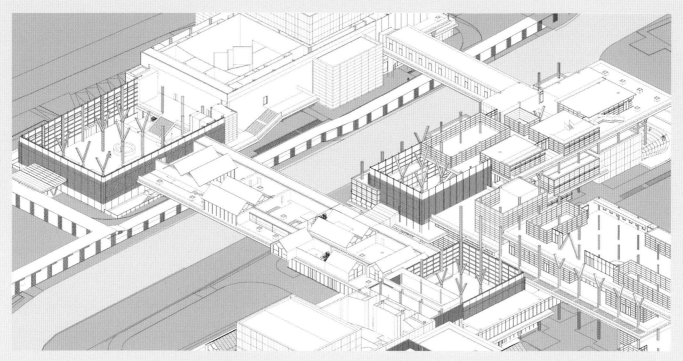
West courtyard

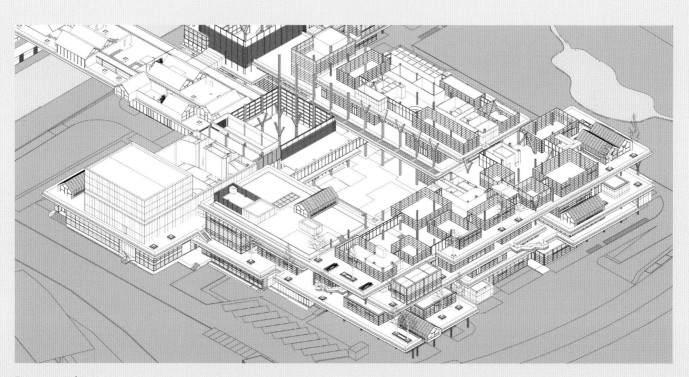
East courtyard

1   100–600 mm lightweight formula planting soil
    20 mm plastic drainage board, topped with polyester needled geotextile moisturizing blanket
    50 mm C20 fine-aggregate concrete as rigid protection layer
    Polyester non-woven fabric barrier
    4 mm high-polymer root puncture-resistant modified asphalt waterproof membrane
    3 mm polymer modified asphalt waterproof membrane
    20 mm cement mortar screed
    Light aggregate concrete slopping with minimum thickness of 30 mm
    130 mm foam glass board
    1.5 mm polymer cement waterproof coating as vapor barrier
    Profiled steel sheet and reinforced-concrete composite slab

2   3 mm wooden textural aluminum panel
    Steel keel
    1 mm galvanized steel sheet
    50 mm rock wool insulation
    Interior decoration layer

3   20-mm-thick 600×1,200 mm precast ceramic tile all-purpose plastic supporter
    40 mm C20 fine-aggregate concrete as rigid protection layer
    Polyester non-woven fabric barrier
    3+3 mm polymer modified asphalt waterproofing membrane
    20 mm cement mortar screed
    Light aggregate concrete slopping with minimum thickness of 30 mm
    130 mm foam glass board
    1.5 mm polymer cement waterproof coating vapor barrier
    Profiled steel sheet and reinforced-concrete composite slab
    Aluminum profile grille ceiling

4   Upper part: Medium-gray aluminum panel
    Middle part: White aluminum panel
    Lower part: Medium-gray aluminum panel

Tree columns and box houses between platforms

Invisible columns merged with façades

The exterior walls of the box houses are aligned with the columns to minimize the columns' footprint in the interior spaces. The view of the column is quartered by the central notches, so as to be similar in size with the window frames. This cloaks the columns within the façades.

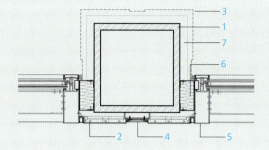

Middle column and exterior wall

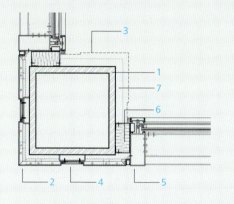

Corner column and exterior wall

1	Steel column
2	3 mm aluminum panel
3	Interior decoration layer
4	Aluminum notch cover
5	Aluminum mullion
6	Rock wool insulation
7	20 mm fireproof paint

Tree and sunlight

The indoor and outdoor Y-columns support the skylights and canopies like tree branches. Four Y-columns are arranged in a spiral pattern to present a visual metaphor of a forest canopy. The skylights also replicate the spiral pattern to form an asymmetrical configuration composed of multiple triangles. Affixed below the skylight, translucent membranes cover the steel structure above and soften the sunlight, so that lighting in the interior is pleasant without harsh flashes.

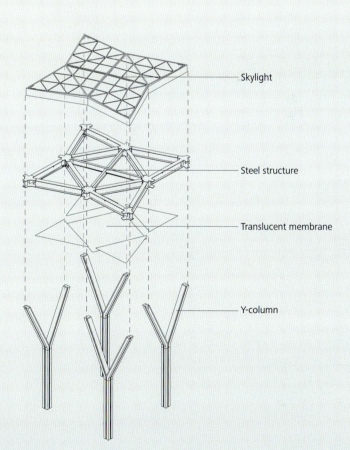

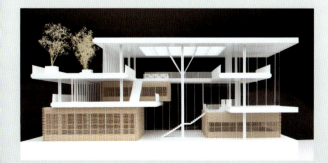

1   3 mm aluminum panel
    6.0 mm ventilation and noise reduction mesh
    3.0 mm self-adhesive waterproof membrane
    0.8 mm galvanized steel sheet leveling blanket
    0.6 mm profiled steel sheet
    130 mm rock wool insulation
    Galvanized steel purlin
    Steel structure

2   Upper part: 3 mm aluminum panel
                Steel keel
                6 mm anti-crack mortar
                50 mm rock wool
                20 mm cement mortar screed
                Mortar, machine sprayed and brushed
                Brick wall
    Middle part: Low-iron insulated low-E glass with wooden textural
                 aluminum frame
    Lower part: Same as upper part

3   Stainless-steel handrail and steel mesh

4   Upper part: 3 mm wooden textural aluminum panel
                Steel keel
                1 mm galvanized steel sheet
                50 mm rock wool
                Interior decoration layer
    Middle part: Low-iron laminated thermal low-E glass with wooden
                 textural aluminum frame
    Lower part: 3 mm wooden textural aluminum panel
                Steel keel
                1 mm galvanized steel sheet
                50 mm rock wool insulation
                Aerated concrete block wall
                Interior decoration layer

5   15 mm reinforced wood composite strip flooring, back brushed with
    anticorrosive and fireproof coating, with louver air outlets near walls
    20 mm cement mortar screed
    Profiled steel sheet and reinforced-concrete composite slab

Garden platform bridge = truss structure + courtyard + corridor + cottage settlement

The garden platform bridge, which extends across the river, is overhung by two major steel trusses and five secondary trusses. These trusses are hidden in walls that shape a group of courtyards and cottages along the bridge.

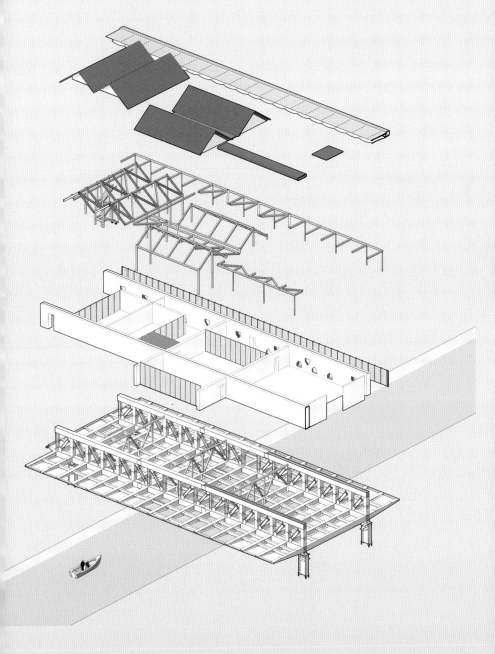

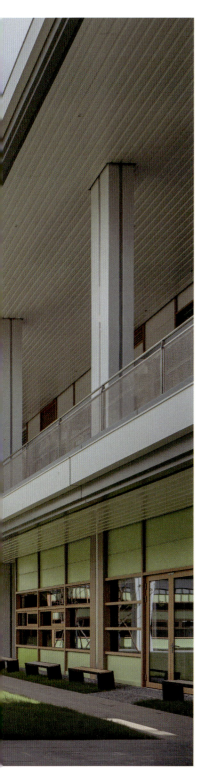

101

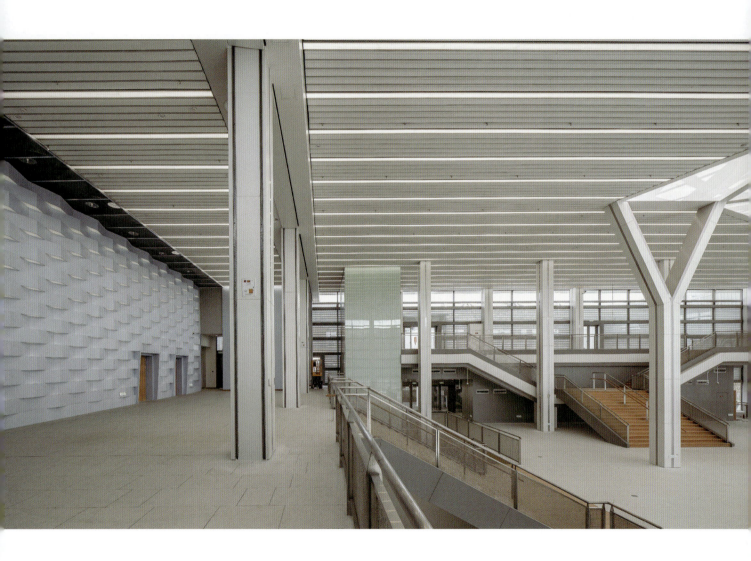

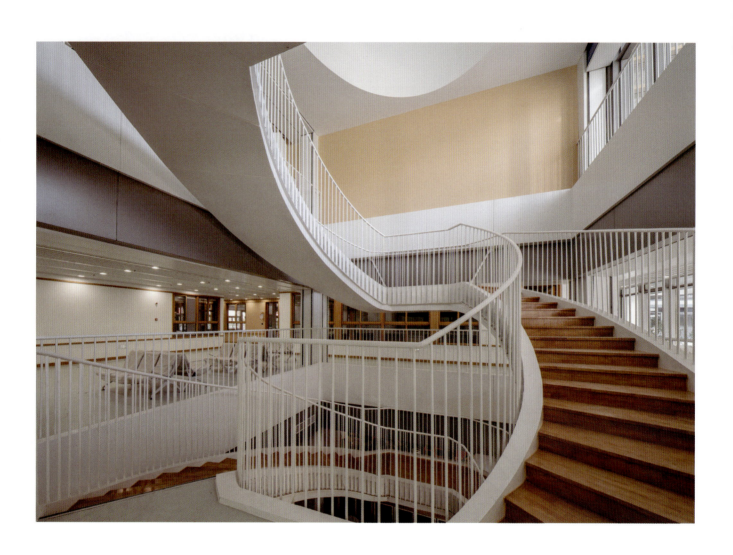

Cells are the basic units of life

Comparing with the basic units of architectural form-type

Cells allow us to gain new insights

Fascinated by the structural order and the inherent space

Fascinated by the permeability and closure of boundaries

Just like inside a living being

Seeing the reproduction of cells

Feeling the flow of energy

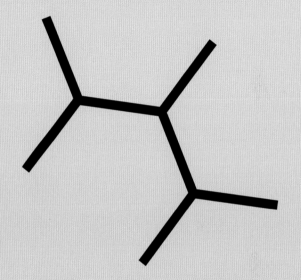

FREE CELL

Natural scenery

Scenery extraction

Scenery-collecting cells

Community Pavilion at Jintao Village

Scene Collector

Location | Dayu Village, Jiading District, Shanghai, China
Program | Community services
Site area | 2,756 ft² (256 m²)
Gross floor area | 2,519 ft² (234 m²)
Designed/built | 2009/2010
Design team | Zhu Xiaofeng, Ding Penghua
Client | Dayu Village Committee
Structural system | Masonry bearing wall and steel structure roof
Main materials | Bare concrete, blue-black brick, China fir panel, aluminum plate, and blue-black tile

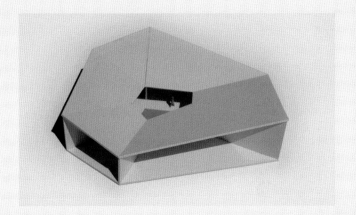

Surrounded by rivers and beautiful bamboo trees, Jintao Village in rural Shanghai is a traditional village in southeast Yangtze River Delta.

The village's community pavilion is located in a barnyard that sits by a river's mouth. The site embodies dual spatial characteristics of openness and aggregation, and we boldly declare these positive attributes through a hexagon-shaped building where residents can rest, recreate, and interact. Within the hexagon, six radial bearing walls define six spaces, three of which are interior spaces containing a recreation room, a teahouse, and a mini stage angled toward the barnyard. The other three are semi-outdoor spaces that face three different sceneries: the stone bridge, the fork of the river, and the concrete bridge. At the center of these six spaces is a courtyard that inherently enhances the configuration. In upholding the tradition of tectonic, the roof slopes inward to drip rainwater runoff into the unique hexagon-shaped courtyard.

The pavilion is designed as a flexible spatial cluster with six homogeneous spaces, in spite of their functional and indoor–outdoor differences. The multipurpose, flexible nature of the spaces reflects the informal rural life of the village. The pavilion also stands as a "scene collector" prototype, and to ensure that locals can identify with the architectural story, we present this prototype with traditional construction methods. The structural system is composed of bar foundations, concrete pedestals, masonry bearing walls, and a steel structure roof. The material language is iterated through blue-black bricks, light-weight partitions, China fir ceilings, and traditional roof tiles. These construction methods and material language reflect the combination of tectonic logic with traditional local style. In placing walls between the pedestal and roof, we gesture to the introduction of a new spatial prototype.

The pavilion has become a popular spot for the locals and they use the space often, embracing it as their main stomping ground, as they partake in many of their favorite activities here. They can be seen relaxing, gathering to chat, reading, playing *mahjong*, and enjoying the many exhibitions and shows held there. A small Osmanthus tree has been planted in the courtyard. We expect it will be well-nurtured and will blossom into a beautiful, iconic tree that will offer shelter to the pavilion and the villagers, as well as provide many sweet and scented memories to all around in the years ahead.

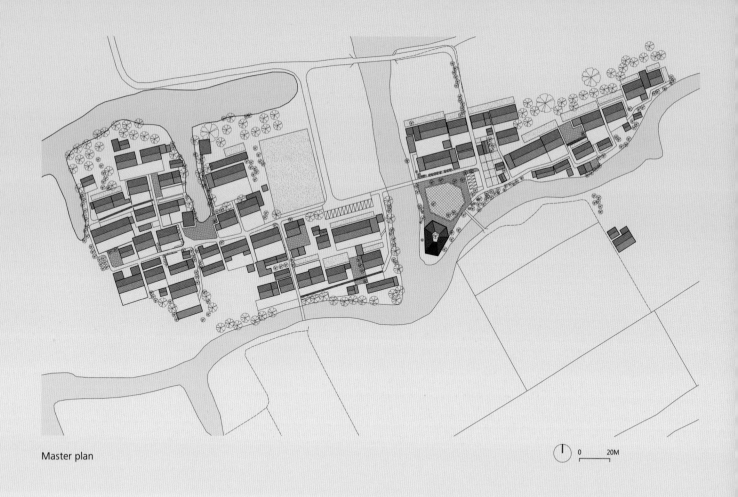
Master plan

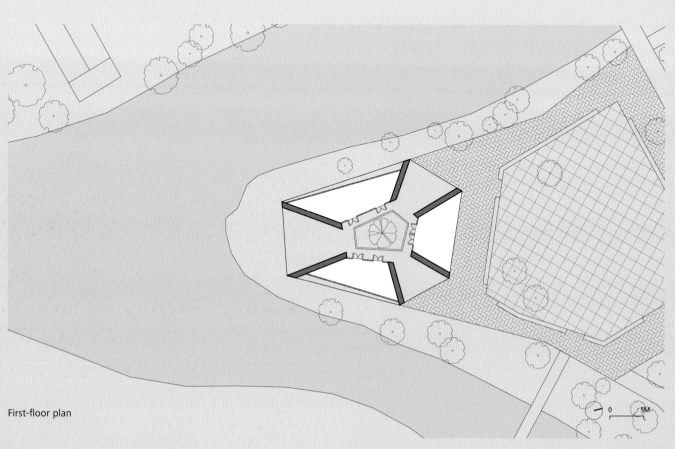
First-floor plan

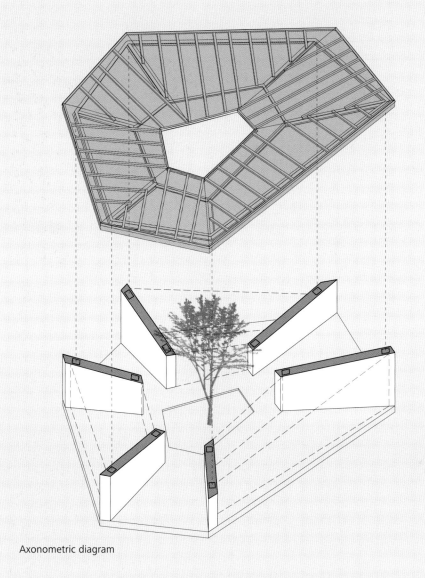

Axonometric diagram

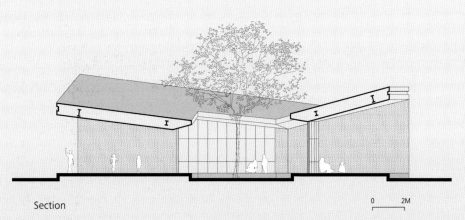

Section

0 2M

1. Chinese-style blue-black tile
   20 mm waterproof membrane
   20 mm timber board
   Steel purlin
   Steel beam
   Pinewood board ceiling

2. 5 mm steel channel

3. Drip joint
   50×50 mm pinewood board cornice

4. Exterior pinewood board
   XPS insulation board
   Interior pinewood board

5. 20 mm 1:2 troweled cement mortar
   Cement flour with suitable amount of water
   1:4 cement mortar binder
   1.5 mm polyurethane waterproof layer
   Cement mortar with construction adhesive
   60 mm C15 concrete subbase
   150 mm 3:7 gray soil
   Packed soil

6. 120 mm tile
   20 mm 1:4 cement mortar bind layer
   60 mm C15 concrete subbase
   150 mm 3:7 gray soil
   Packed soil

7. Blue-black brick

Thick and thin cornices

Outer cornice

The outer cornice is thick, emphasizing the volume of the roof. The China fir cladding that is on the underside of the outer cornice is also the ceiling material. This intensifies the continuity of the ceiling and makes distinct the orientation of the radial spaces.

Inner cornice

The ceiling under the inner eaves slopes up toward the cornice to reduce the thickness of the inner cornice, so that it's similar to a traditional Chinese cornice. Traditional drip tiles on the roof direct rainwater into a central water collection in the courtyard. The water is drained out through ducts to irrigate the trees in the courtyard. This revives the traditional concept of "gathering water from all sides to the central courtyard."

The spaces' flexible and multipurpose nature is a reflection of the informal rural life.

The pavilion is designed as a flexible spatial cluster and presents itself suitably as a "scene collector" prototype.

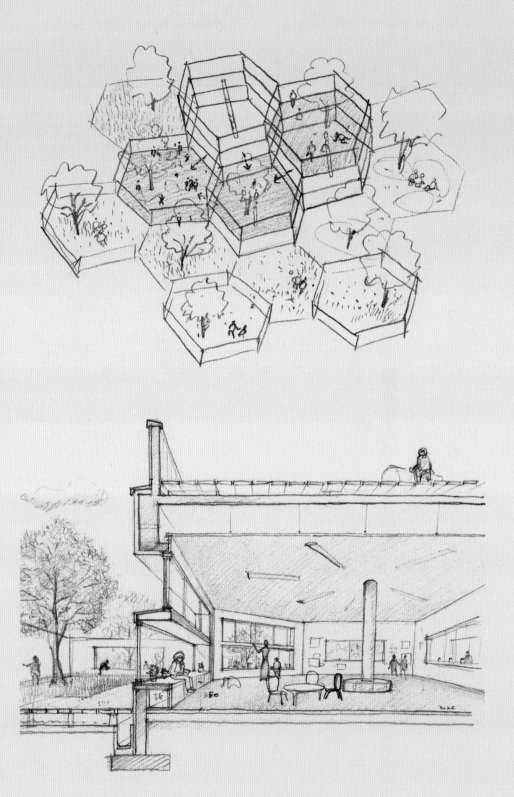

Bilingual Kindergarten Affiliated to East China Normal University

Childhood in a Honeycomb

Location | Anting Town, Jiading District, Shanghai, China
Program | Kindergarten (with fifteen classes)
Site area | 79,653 ft² (7,400 m²)
Gross floor area | 71,042 ft² (6,600 m²)
Designed/built | 2012/2015
Design team | Zhu Xiaofeng, Li Qitong, Ding Penghua, Yang Hong, Du Jie, Shi Yan'an, Cai Mian, Du Shigang, Jiang Meng, Hu Qiming, Guo Ying
Client | Shanghai International Automobile City Group Co. Ltd
Local design institute | Shanghai Jiangnan Architectural Design Institution Co. Ltd
Structural system | Reinforced-concrete framework and steel framework (part of the corridors)
Main materials | White fluorocarbon paint, transparent and fritted glass, aluminum profile, and plastic-wood composite flooring

In traditional Chinese architecture, courtyards bring people together and help maintain close ties between family members, and strengthen relationships with friends and relatives. They also present a physical avenue to connect with nature and the benevolent vibrations of the Universe's omnipresent energy. Unfortunately, today, this connection has become almost impossible in most urban households within densely populated metropolises. The kindergarten's site is of modest size, located in a new neighborhood in Anting Town, Shanghai. Instead of designing tedious rectangular blocks that would house children and teachers in classrooms confined in a linear arrangement, we sought to provide dynamic class units with courtyards. Such a design provides a nurturing environment where the children can observe nature, and be acquainted with the customs and etiquettes of society through interaction and play.

Taking inspiration from the angled western borderline of the site, we organized the plan in a terraced "W" shape to capture maximum sunlight from the south, east, and west. From past experiences, and analyses, we have discovered that hexagonal units and honeycomb compositions can better fit the turns and bends of the "W" shape and create more dynamic and aggregated indoor and outdoor spaces, which would also successfully avoid the axisymmetric solemnity of a traditional quadrangle. Our design panned out in irregular hexagonal units for each classroom and courtyard—only three sides of the hexagon are composed in equal lengths—enabling a flexible combination that accommodates various functions, while optimizing sunlight conditions.

Past the main gate, zigzag corridors lead the children along the hexagons' perimeter to the entrance courtyard and lobby. The paths then fork and reconnect at different points, allowing cheerful intervals of flowers and trees in different courtyards to greet the students on their way to their classrooms. Activities in the classrooms are conducted around the central column; bay window spaces can be utilized to read, draw, or even set up a window-sill potted-plant garden. Every two classrooms share a courtyard, with direct indoor and outdoor connections, and when children leave their own courtyard to go to other areas, like the library, music room, art room, canteen, multifunction room, or small farm, they enjoy engaging journeys, filled with discovery and amusement, moving along the many winding routes in this hexagonal "honeycomb" maze. They can also conveniently join activities held at the big playground that is connected through outdoor staircases. By connecting multiple interior and exterior spaces of varying scales along the routes, we provide children with opportunities to discover nature and get familiar with day-to-day cultural norms. We believe that these experiences of exploring, observing, and communicating in the "honeycomb" will enrich their education and become a part of their childhood memories to treasure.

Master plan

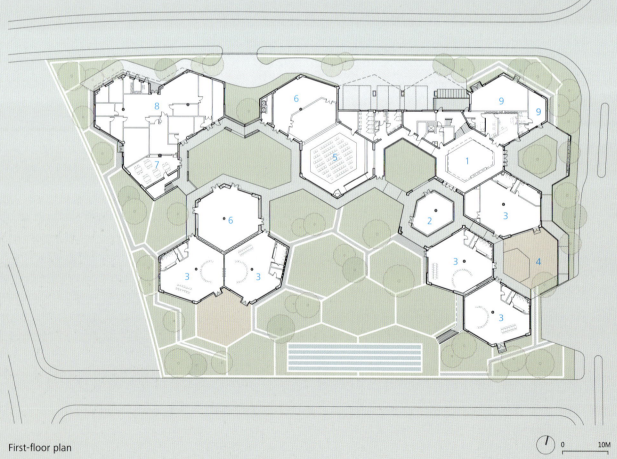

First-floor plan

1 Lobby
2 Nursery classroom
3 Classroom
4 Outdoor activity platform
5 Multifunction room
6 Activity room
7 Canteen
8 Kitchen
9 Service room
10 Library
11 Office

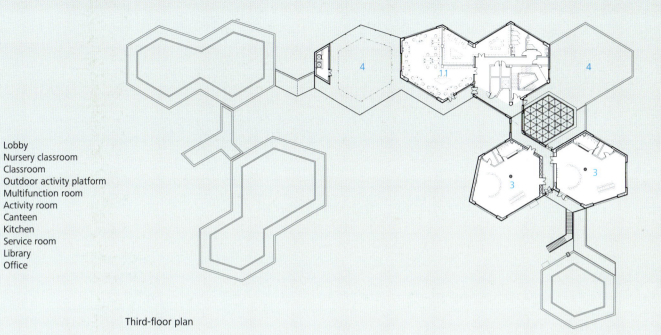

Third-floor plan

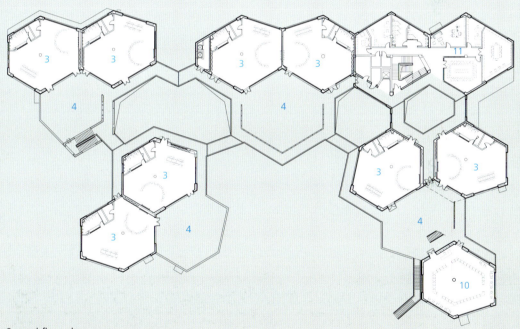

Second-floor plan

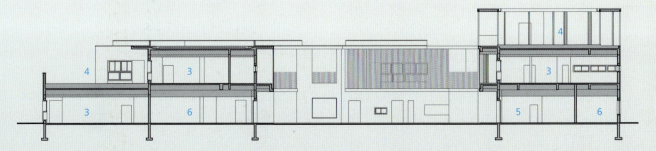

Section

Inside/outside of recessed/bay window

1. 30 mm layer of pebble with grain size φ15
   40 mm C20 fine-aggregate concrete protection layer
   10 mm lime mortar barrier
   2.5 mm polymer waterproof membrane (two layers)
   1 mm coated plastic vapor barrier
   20 mm 1:3 cement mortar screed
   105 mm foam glass insulation board
   Ceramsite aggregate concrete sloping (minimal thickness of 30 mm)
   Cast-in-place reinforced-concrete slab brushed with cement paste

2. White fluorocarbon paint
   Water-based waterproof primer
   Elastic primer, flexible water-resistant putty
   6 mm mortar screed with internal alkali-resistant glass fiber mesh cloth
   70 mm foam glass insulation board

   2 mm binder
   5 mm polymer cement waterproof mortar
   20 mm 1:3 cement mortar screed with steel mesh inside
   Porous concrete wall

3. 25 mm plastic-wood composite flooring
   50×50 mm secondary wood stud @<400
   60×90 mm or 50×50 mm main wood stud @<1200
   Hollow, higher than 20 mm
   200×200 mm brick block @<1800, fastened to anticorrosive timber blocking
   40 mm C20 fine-aggregate concrete protection layer
   10 mm lime mortar barrier
   2.5 mm high polymer waterproof membrane (two layers)
   1 mm coated plastic vapor barrier
   20 mm 1:3 cement mortar screed
   105 mm foam glass insulation board

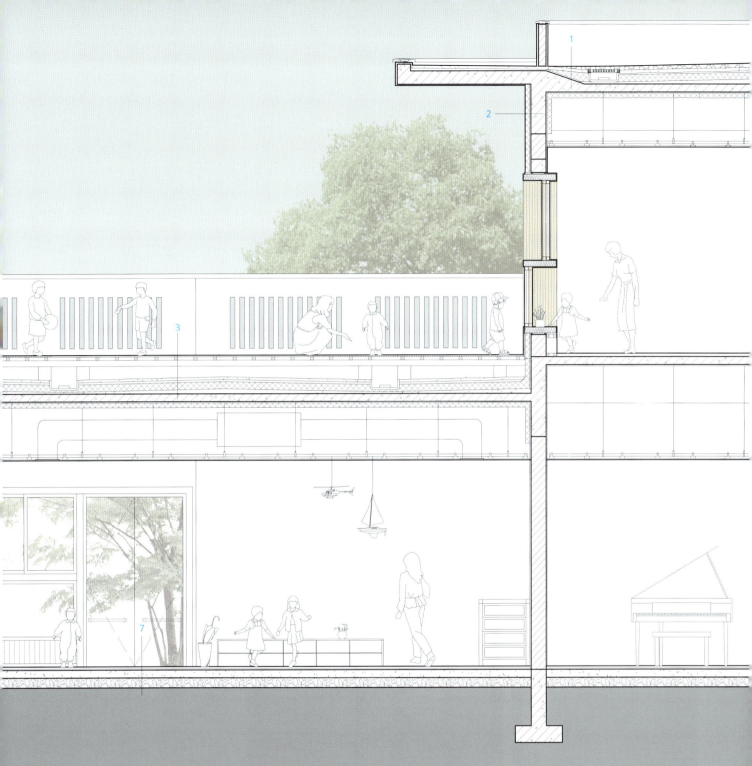

    Ceramsite aggregate concrete sloping (minimal thickness of 30 mm)
    Cast-in-place reinforced-concrete slab brushed with cement mortar

4   20x100 mm wooden textural aluminum profile
    40x40 mm hot-dip galvanized square steel pipe
    5 mm polymer cement waterproof mortar
    20 mm 1:3 cement mortar screed
    Cast-in-place reinforced-concrete beam

5   Recessed window (only operated by teachers)
    3 mm wood-textural aluminum panel
    Steel beams with 70 mm semi-rigid foam glass insulation board in between
    10 mm interior wood decoration board

6   Bay window (used by kids), with details the same as No. 5

7   4 mm environmentally friendly linoleum flooring, bound by construction adhesive
    Cement paste
    30 mm 1:2.5 cement mortar screed
    Cast-in-place reinforced-concrete floor slab

Children's bay window and teachers' recessed window

The windows in classrooms are composed of two parts. The lower part is a bay window with fixed casements and an 11.8-inch-high (300-millimeter-high) window seat. This provides children with unique, cave-like spaces to play, read, and even set up a potted-plant garden. The upper part forms recessed casement windows that can be easily opened and operated by teachers.

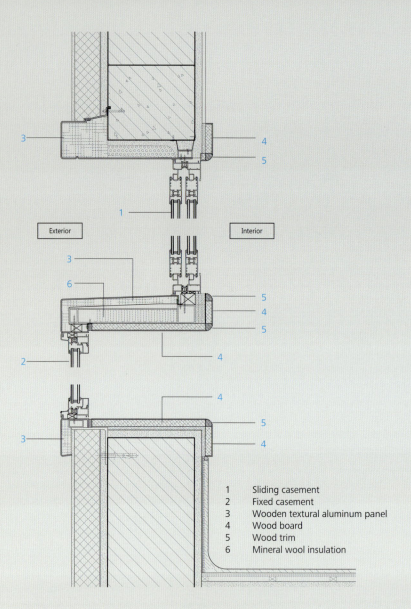

1	Sliding casement
2	Fixed casement
3	Wooden textural aluminum panel
4	Wood board
5	Wood trim
6	Mineral wool insulation

Classrooms with courtyards

Each hexagonal classroom unit projects a sense of centrality: the central pillar emphasizes the hexagon's cohesiveness and encourages users to arrange the surrounding space in a flexible way.

First-floor classrooms and courtyard

Every two classrooms share a courtyard, which provides a fun outdoor space that encourages interaction, play, and fellowship and unity between the students. The terraced design of the courtyards also creates opportunities for students to observe their friends and the activities within other courtyards, providing opportunities for a friendly wave or greeting through these chance encounters.

Second-floor classrooms and courtyard

The combination of classroom unit and courtyard encourages children to observe nature and get familiarized with day-to-day culture, as they are also shaped through rich interactions.

We believe that the many experiences of exploring, observing, and communicating in the "honeycomb" will become a part of precious childhood memories.

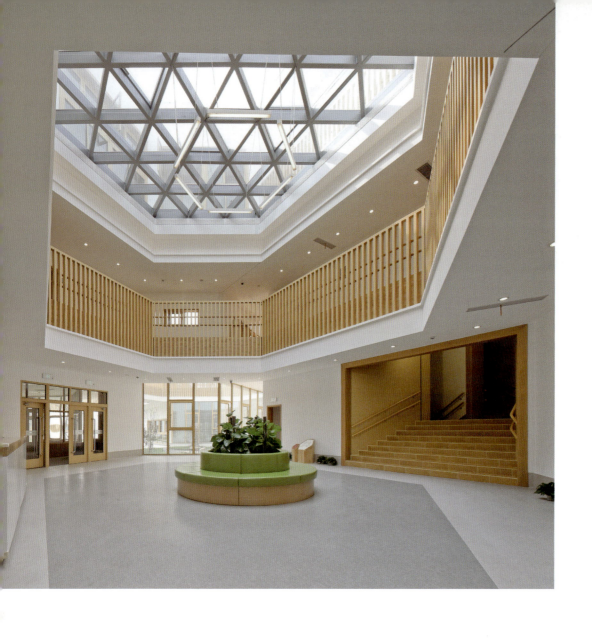

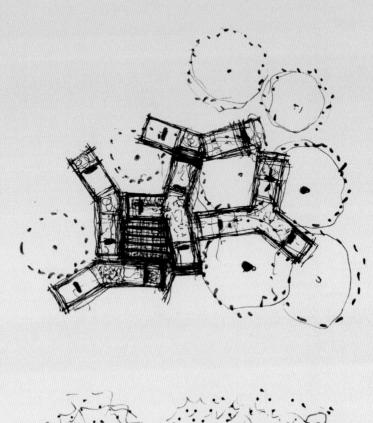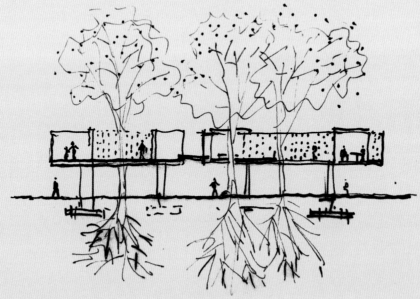

Shanghai Google Creators' Society Center

Floating Among Trees

Location | Guiling Road and Yishan Road, Xuhui District, Shanghai, China
Program | Exhibition center, science and culture communication, and teahouse
Site area | 20,494 ft² (1,904 m²)
Gross floor area | 7,857 ft² (730 m²)
Designed/built | 2012/2013
Design team | Zhu Xiaofeng, Ding Penghua, Cai Mian, Yang Hong
Client | China Fortune Properties
Structure Design | Greenland Steel Structure
Landscape design | DLC Landscape
Structural system | SRC and steel truss
Main materials | Mirror-finish stainless steel, twisted and tensioned aluminum strips, transparent and fritted glass, solid and perforated aluminum panel, gravel, and water

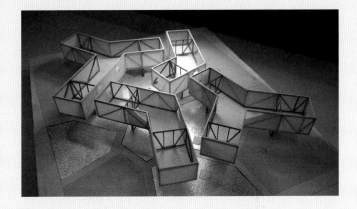

Located along a main road in southwest downtown Shanghai, the site, which is home to six aged camphor trees, is an uplifting "green" thoroughfare utilized by citizens. The openness of the area and the trees at the site inspired the starting point of the design concept, which branched into two main strategies: elevate the main volume of the building to the second floor, so as to maximize the open ground space, and protect the thriving trees on the site, as well as establish an intimate and interactive relationship with them.

The center showcases four independently suspended structures linked to one another by bridges. Ten pieces of reinforced-concrete walls that route vertical MEP ducts support these suspended structures—almost like tree trunks that support far-reaching branches and supply nutrition to these branches and leaves. The walls on the first floor are wrapped in reflective, stainless-steel panels and are cleverly camouflaged to reflect the surrounding green environment, making them dissolve into a scenery of trees. This exaggerates the openness of the ground space and enhances the floating effect of the upper volumes. An atrium on the first floor, enclosed by transparent curtain walls, persuades the eye toward the stunning skylight above. The design invites natural light into the area with enthusiasm, as it promotes a fluid connection between indoor and outdoor spaces.

Four floating volumes supported by steel trusses weave in between the old camphor trees and stretch horizontally in a "Y" and "L" formation. A twisted-strip aluminum skin composes a translucent façade and shapes a series of interior and exterior spaces. This "twisted" design narration also aids to present the truss structure behind vaguely, rather than conspicuously.

Wandering among the maze of these translucent walls, visitors encounter an alternation of courtyards, bridges, and pockets of refreshing nature. This interaction of nature, tectonics, time, and space come through seamlessly in this iconic project that presents the successful collaboration of architecture and nature.

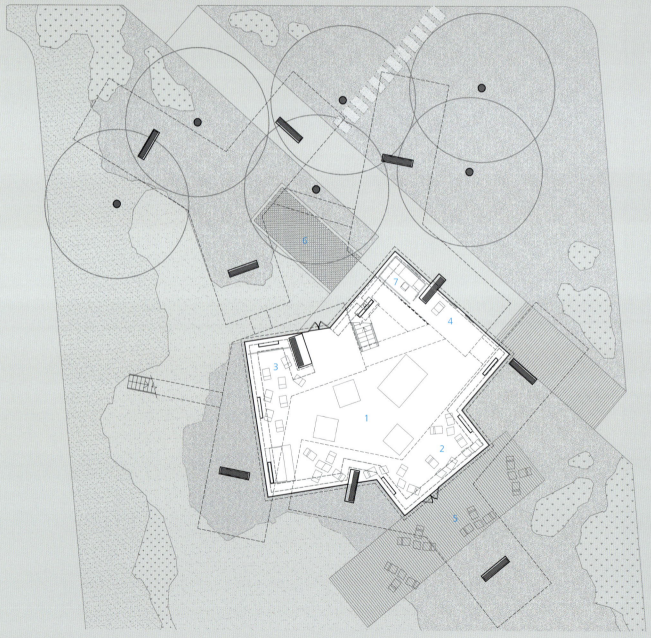

First-floor plan

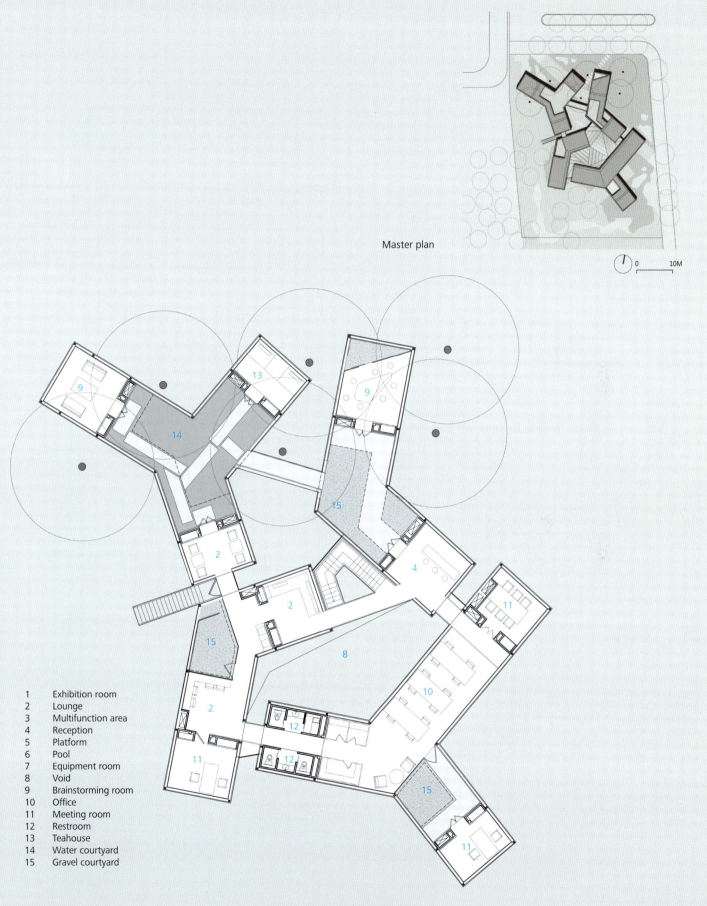

Master plan

1 Exhibition room
2 Lounge
3 Multifunction area
4 Reception
5 Platform
6 Pool
7 Equipment room
8 Void
9 Brainstorming room
10 Office
11 Meeting room
12 Restroom
13 Teahouse
14 Water courtyard
15 Gravel courtyard

Second-floor plan

Section

1	Exhibition room
2	Office
3	Gravel courtyard
4	Meeting room
5	Water courtyard
6	Pool

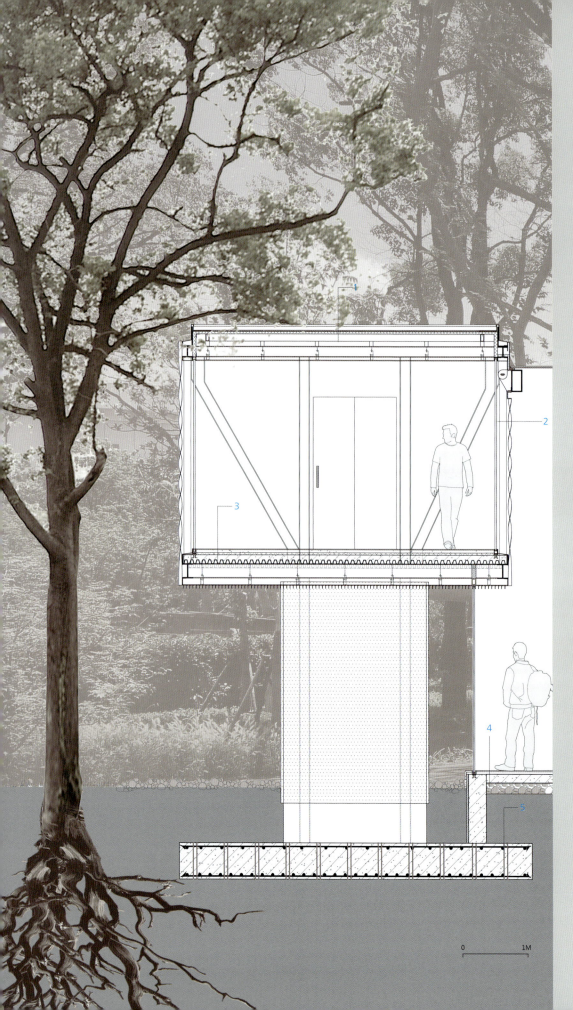

1 Asphalt tile
  3 mm APP modified waterproof bituminous membrane
  50 mm steel coreboard

2 Twisted and tensioned aluminum strips
  Insulated glass door and window

3 Impregnated protective coating
  15 mm colored grindstone
  35 mm fine-aggregate concrete leveling blanket with crossed φ 4 mm rebar @200
  30 mm EPS insulation board
  Profiled steel sheet and reinforced-concrete composite floor slab

4 Impregnated protective coating
  15 mm colored grindstone
  35 mm anti-crack mortar screed
  Cement mortar
  120 mm C20 concrete subbase
  150 mm packed rubble

5 300 mm reinforced-concrete slab foundation
  Rebar
  Embedded permeable PVC tubes

0   1M

Intergrowth with tree

Translucent foundation

To protect the six aged camphor trees on the site, enlarged foundations were buried shallow. Permeable PVC tubes were embedded in the foundation slab to allow rainwater to penetrate to the roots, so that the trees would continue to grow healthily.

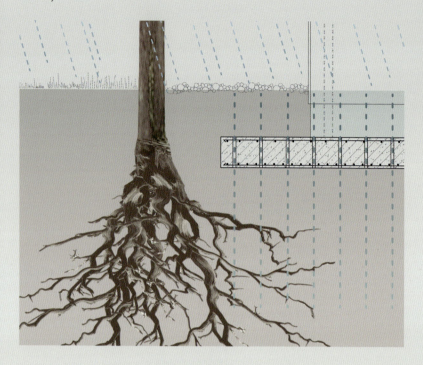

Invisible pillar structure

Ten concrete walls support the upper structures, with pipes and cables installed along them. Wrapped by stainless-steel panels with mirror-finish, the walls hide themselves by reflecting the surrounding greenery, amplifying the openness of the grounds and enhancing the floating effect of the upper volumes.

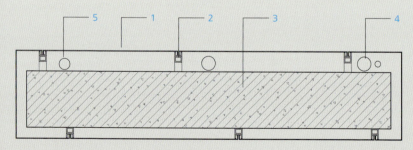

1   Stainless-steel panel with mirror-finish
2   Galvanized steel keel
3   Reinforced-concrete shear wall
4   Drainpipe
5   Electrical wire pipe

Artificial leaves

The façade is dressed in a wavy "skin" of twisted and tensioned aluminum strips inspired by leaves—in the way that they are strong enough to shelter from a harsh sun or drizzle, but also permeable enough to allow through dappled daylight and the gentle caress of a breeze. Fastened securely at the bottom and hinged with an adjustable bolt at the top, each aluminum strip is angled ninety degrees to the next one, forming a rich texture of subtle waves that evoke a play of light and shadow.

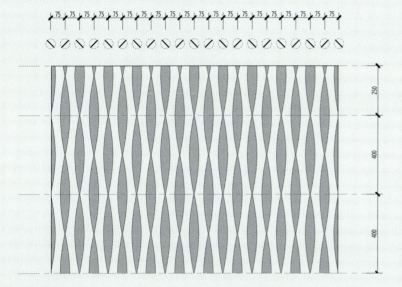

Gravel courtyard and water courtyard

The second floor is a quiet place that is ideal for holding a discussion or simply relaxing. The white gravel in the courtyard decelerates hurried steps and the pond languidly reflects trees and nature; one is urged to slow down, take in the scenery, and contemplate the unusual space. A waterfall cascades from the bridge into a pool on the ground, creating soothing acoustics while improving the microclimate of the environment.

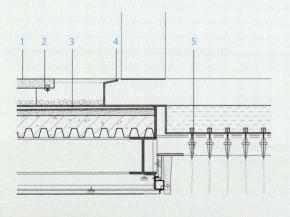

1	Bluestone steps	6	White gravel
2	LED illuminator	7	Stone
3	Stainless-steel basin	8	Steel grating
4	Overflow	9	Drainpipe
5	Waterfall outlet		

Streaming down from the bridge, the waterfall refreshes the ambiance and improves the microclimate of the area as it resonates the calming acoustics of trickling water.

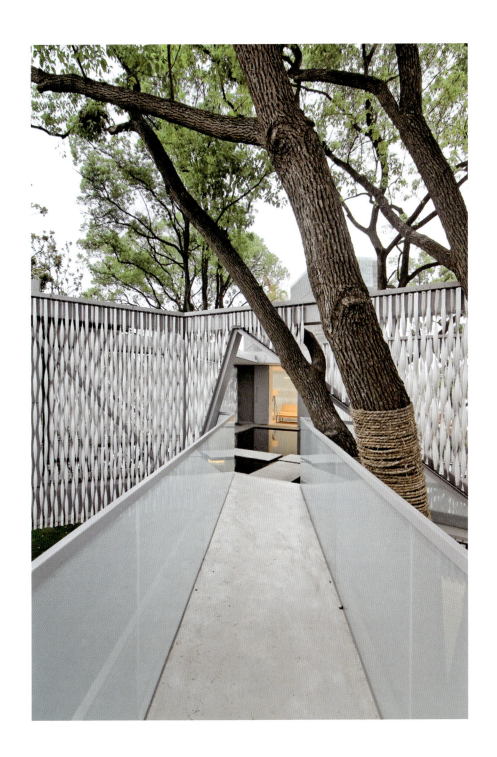

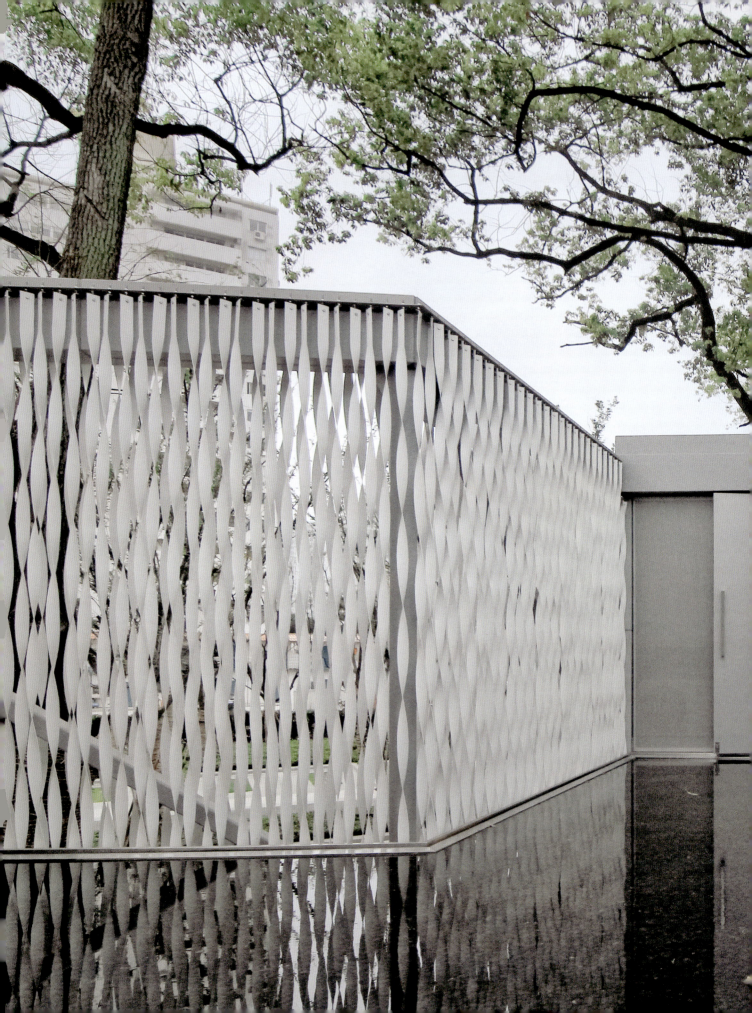

Ten pieces of reinforced-concrete walls support the upper structures and route vertical MEP ducts, just like tree trunks supporting and supplying nutrition to branches and leaves.

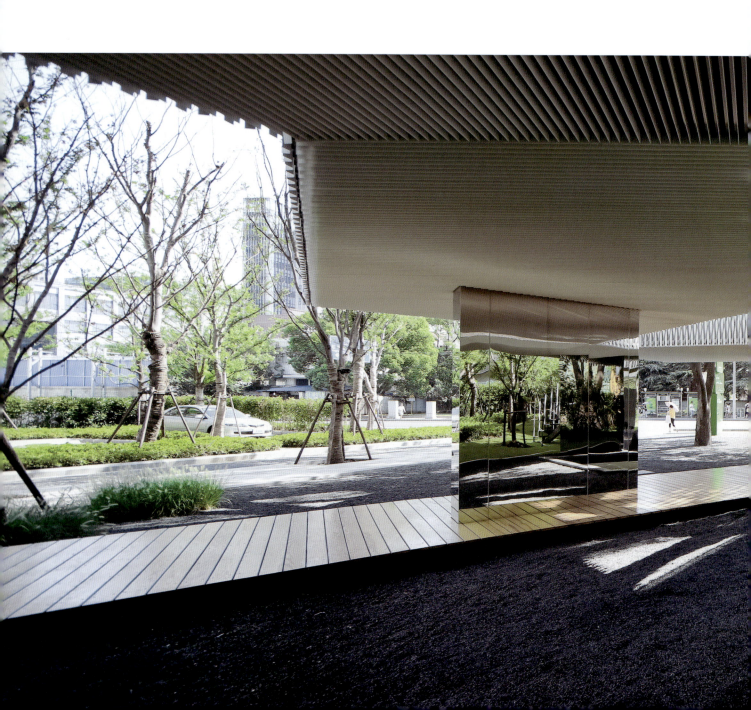

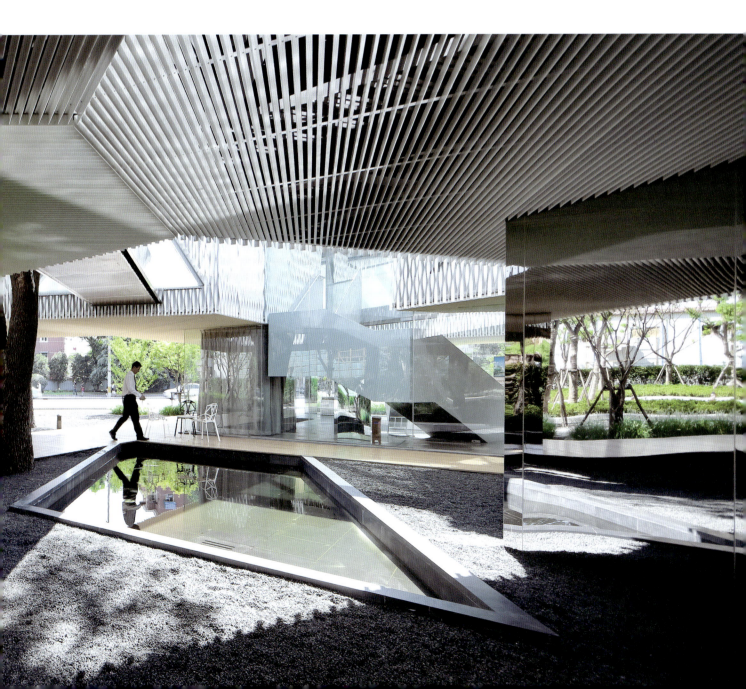

Wandering through the maze of these translucent walls, visitors will encounter courtyards, bridges, and pockets of refreshing nature inspired by an environmental concept that captivates through the interaction of nature, tectonics, time, and space.

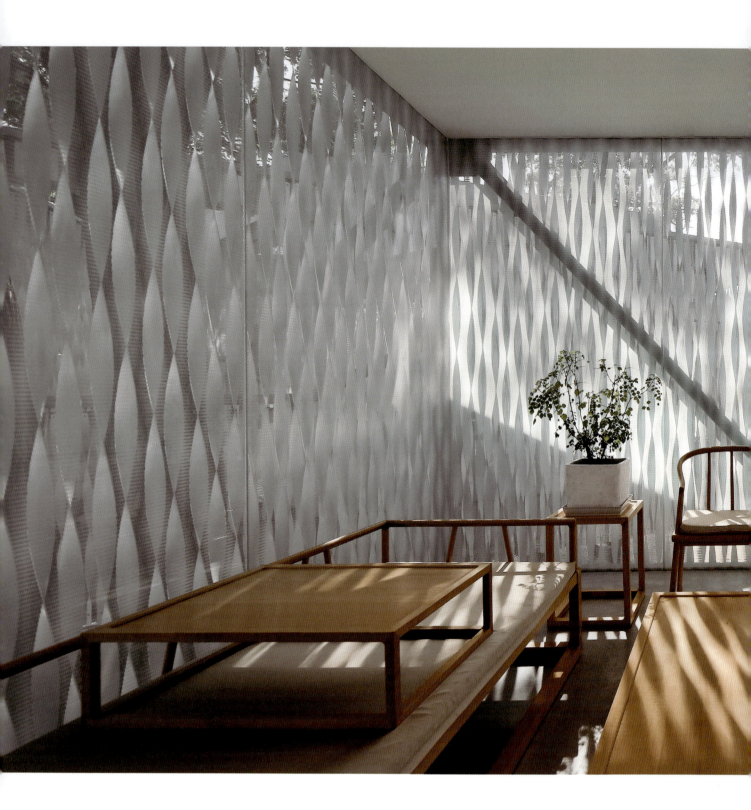

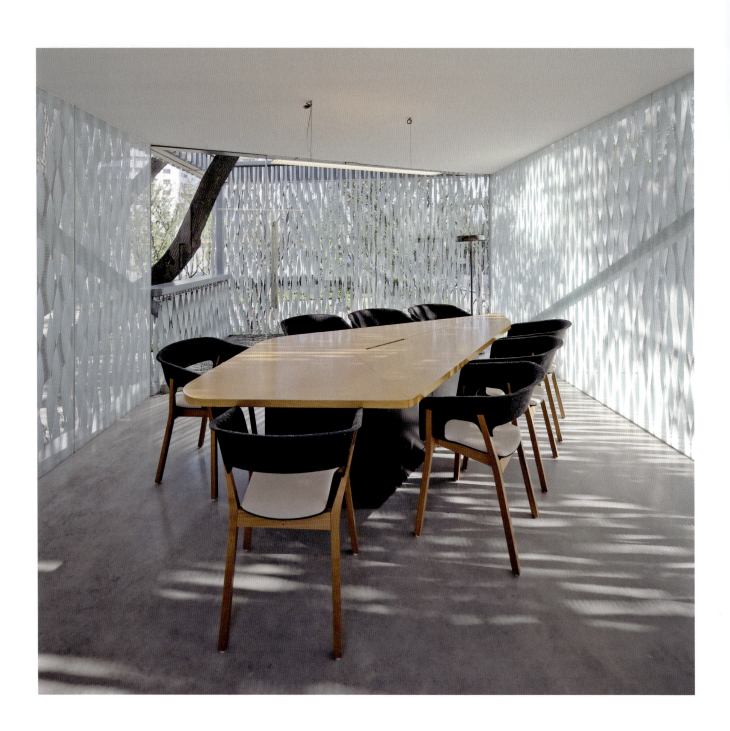

A collaboration of architecture and nature.

177

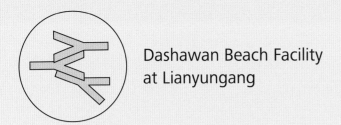

Dashawan Beach Facility at Lianyungang

Enlightenment of Waves

Location | Liandao Island, Lianyungang City, Jiangsu Province, China
Program | Locker and shower facilities, restaurant, gymnasium, recreation centers, and guestrooms
Site area | 223,437 ft² (20,758 m²)
Gross floor area | 83,539 ft² (7,761 m²)
Designed/built | 2007/2009
Design team | Zhu Xiaofeng, Cai Jiangsi, Xu Lei, Xu Ye, Ding Xufen
Client | Liandao Seafront Resort Committee
Local design institute | Shanghai Archin (International) Design Consultants Pte Ltd
Structural system | Reinforced-concrete framework
Main materials | Bare concrete, insulated glass, and anticorrosive timber floor

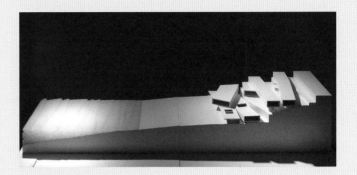

Facing the east of the Pacific Ocean, the site is located on one of the islands of Lianyungang, Jiangsu Province, Shanghai, an emerging harbor city along the China coastline. The resort's beach hosts about 20,000 swimmers per day during peak hours in the summer. To meet the needs of an increasing crowd, we were commissioned to design a new beach facility that would house shower facilities, restaurants, a gymnasium, recreation centers, and accommodations.

Situated on a sloping mountain outcropping that rolls out to the beach, the building is designed in a terrace layout, so that visitors can enjoy the beautiful panoramic views from every level. Integrated into the natural slope, the building becomes a part of the mountain that trails to the beach and the sea beyond. We drew inspiration from the vitality of the waves—in how they endlessly overlap and chase each other—and lent this dynamism to the design. We created three Y-shaped units that are stacked freely, and which stretch out three-dimensionally. These units, which accommodate the three main functions—shower areas, restaurants, and guestrooms—provide interactions between different circulations and create various spatial experiences on and below the roof. "Enlightened" by waves, the design breaks from the conventional definition of building levels and creates a playful relationship between the architectural units.

Bare concrete is chosen as the main material for the façades to present a rough texture that matches the beach and the mountain backdrop. A sand finish on the roof of the shower rooms also echoes the spirit and scenery of the beach. Higher up ground, the roof lawn mimics the coastal mountain grass and is trimmed by a wooden deck that evokes a relaxed atmosphere and a resort ambiance. In the locker rooms and shower area, glass bricks and hidden skylights introduce daylight from the outside and stitch a dazzling tapestry of reflections and light. Evolved from archetypal terraced volumes, the Y-shaped units grow and interweave freely in multiple dimensions that dialogue easily with the rocky mountain and fluid ocean. In doing so, they confidently organize the landscape and reconstruct the natural scenery. When the experience of architecture marries with nature, the extraordinary occurs—such that architecture may reconstruct the original scenery and change the way and the scenario in which nature is perceived.

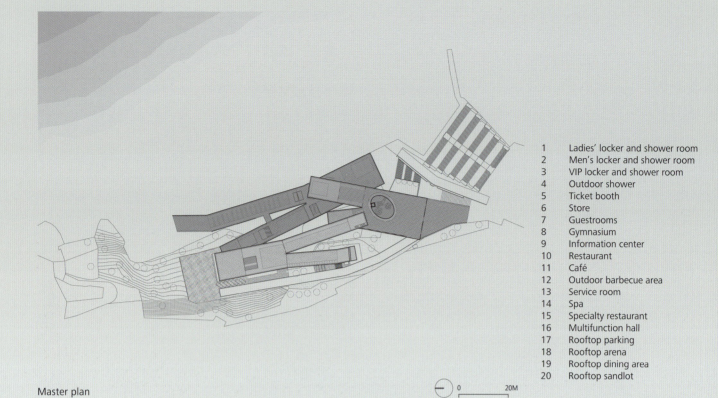

Master plan

1	Ladies' locker and shower room
2	Men's locker and shower room
3	VIP locker and shower room
4	Outdoor shower
5	Ticket booth
6	Store
7	Guestrooms
8	Gymnasium
9	Information center
10	Restaurant
11	Café
12	Outdoor barbecue area
13	Service room
14	Spa
15	Specialty restaurant
16	Multifunction hall
17	Rooftop parking
18	Rooftop arena
19	Rooftop dining area
20	Rooftop sandlot

Lower-level plan

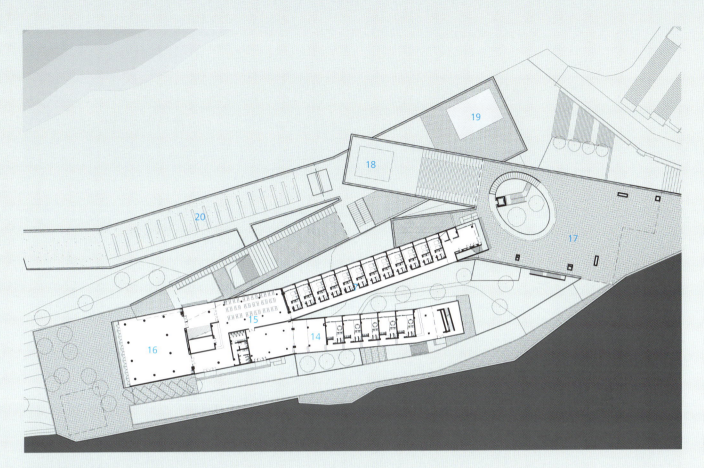
Upper-level plan

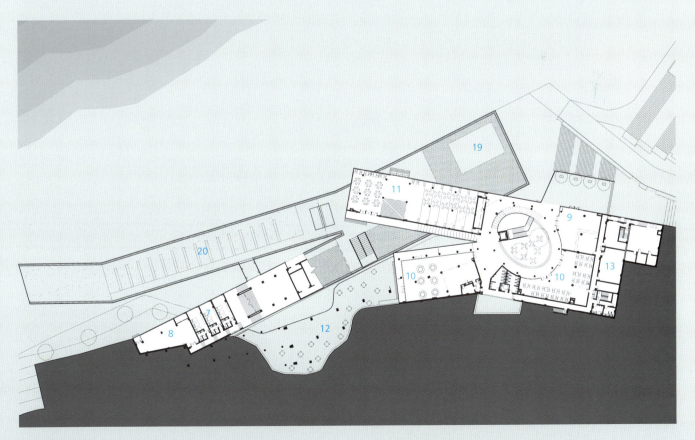
Middle-level plan

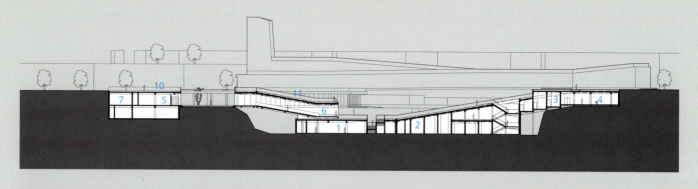
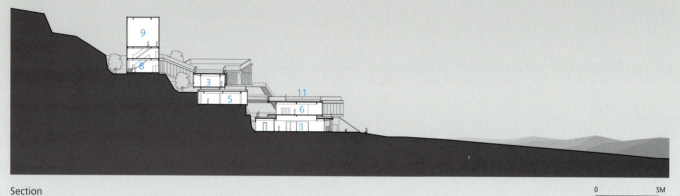

Section

1	Men's locker and shower room	7	Service room
2	VIP locker and shower room	8	Spa
3	Guestrooms	9	Specialty restaurant
4	Gymnasium	10	Rooftop parking
5	Restaurant	11	Rooftop arena
6	Café		

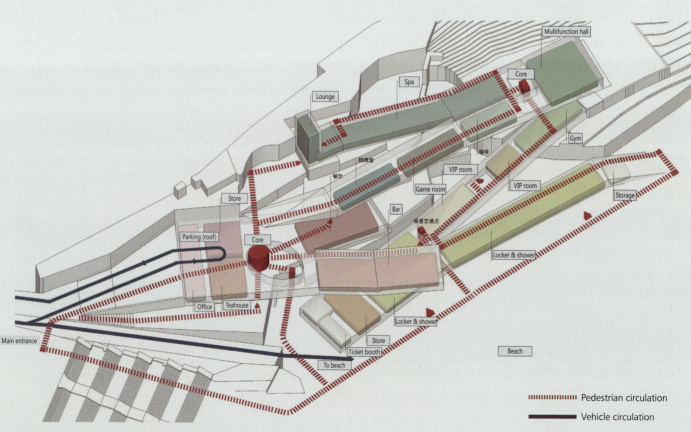

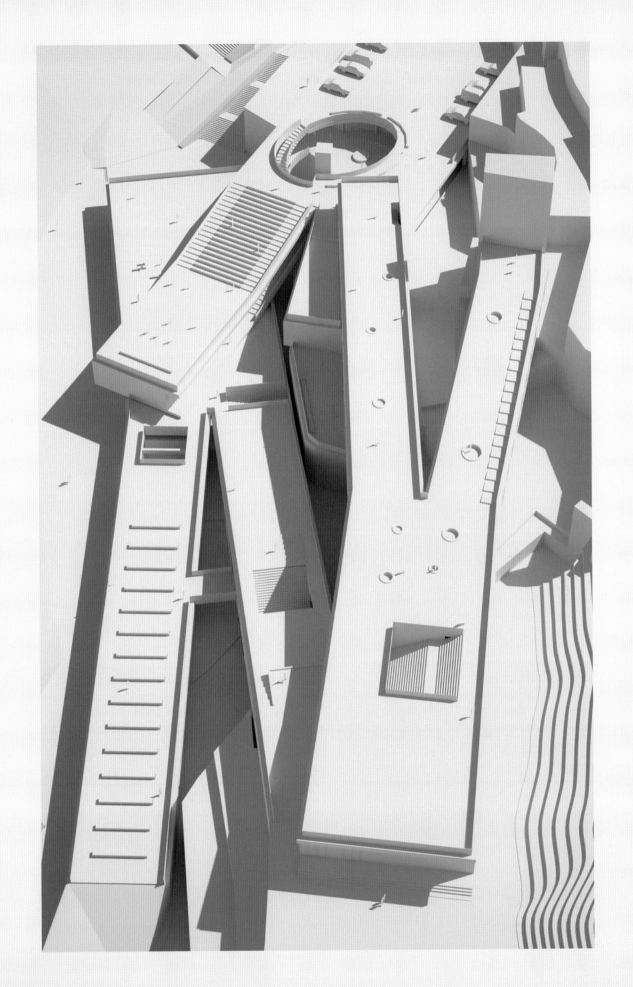

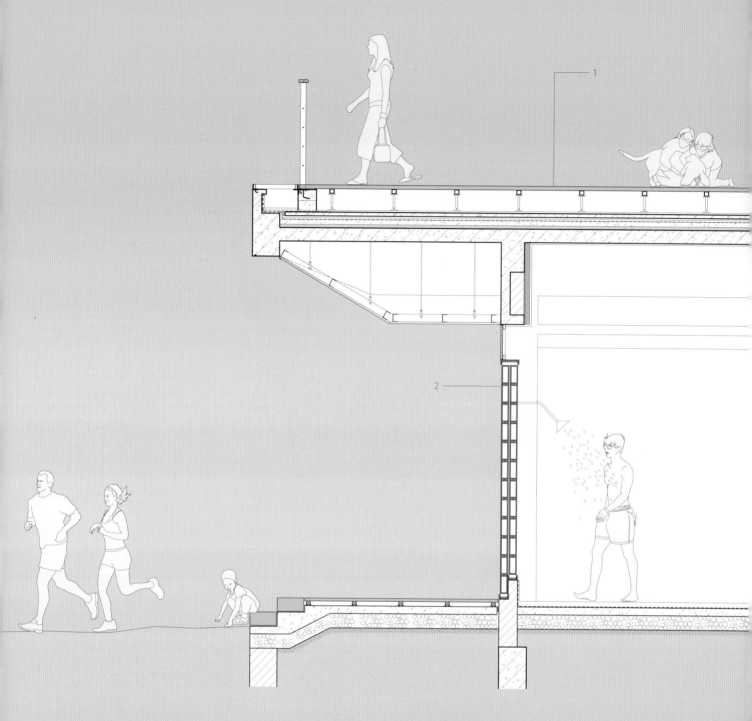

1 Anticorrosive timber flooring
Hollow
40 mm fine-aggregate concrete waterproof course
8 mm white lime mortar barrier
2 mm polymer modified waterproof bituminous membrane
20 mm 1:3 cement mortar screed
Ceramsite aggregate concrete sloping (minimal thickness of 30 mm)
35 mm XPS foam insulation
Cast-in-place reinforced-concrete slab

2 200 mm glass brick wall
Shower pipes (sandwiched)
200 mm glass brick wall

3 200–300 mm fine sands
Polyester needled geotextile filter
80 mm ϕ15–20 mm pebble drainage layer
40 mm fine-aggregate concrete waterproof course
8 mm white lime mortar barrier
2 mm polymer modified waterproof bituminous membrane
20 mm 1:3 cement mortar screed
Clay aggregate concrete sloping (minimal thickness of 30 mm)
35 mm XPS foam insulation
Cast-in-place reinforced-concrete slab

Seashore energy-saving device

The exterior walls of the shower rooms are double-layered glass brick walls, with shower pipes that run in between. This not only allows sufficient daylight to filter in but also awards privacy and uniqueness to the shower experience. The interior walls are also double-layered, with shower pipes that run in between. Hot and humid air is ventilated out through high windows and the hollow above.

4   5 mm ceramic mosaic with white cement seaming
    3 mm construction adhesive cement mortar binder
    Cement paste
    6 mm cement lime mortar screed
    8 mm cement lime mortar scratch coat
    Water-resistant putty smoothing
    Layer of plastic-coated mesh cloth with adhesive
    Polymer cement mortar
    50 mm reinforced (polymer) cement polyphenol composite board
    10 mm air gap
    Brick wall
    Shower pipes (sandwiched)

When the experience of architecture marries with nature, the extraordinary occurs, such that architecture reconstructs the original scenery, and changes the way and scenario in which nature is perceived.

The design breaks free from the traditional definition, as well as limitation, of stacked building levels and creates a playful relationship between architectural units.

Standing between two large trees

With two branches interlocking overhead

This is the prototype of a human home

Subconscious construction creates subconscious space

Homes give people stability, intimacy, and warmth

We believe

Given today's diversified meaning of space

The notion of home can be endowed with new concepts

The form-type of home can be continuously expanded

To extend itself in the history of humankind

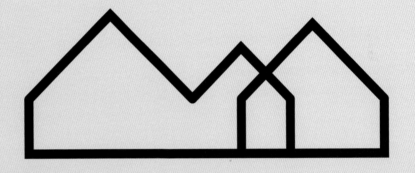

EXTENSION OF HOME

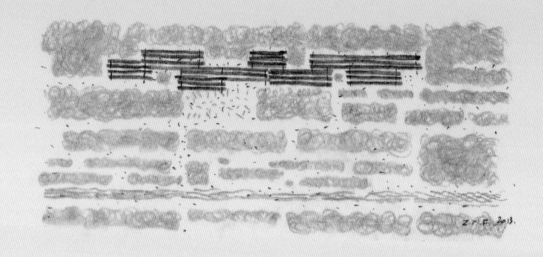

Activity Homes at Yunjin Road

Folded Plates Take-off

Location | No. 280 Yunjin Road, Xuhui District, Shanghai, China
Program | Public facilities and restaurant
Gross floor area | Restaurant: 5,413.2 ft^2 (502.9 m²)
Community pavilion: 5,803.9 ft^2 (539.2 m²)
Coffee shop: 781.5 ft^2 (72.6 m²)
Designed/built | 2014/2018
Design team | Zhu Xiaofeng, Zhuang Xinjia (project manager), Jiang Meng (project architect), Pablo Gonzalez Riera, Shi Yan'an, Du Shigang, Sheng Tai
Client | Xuhui Riverfront Development Investment and Construction Ltd
Structural consultant | Zhang Zhun (AND Office)
Local design institute | Shanghai Municipal Engineering Design Institute (Group) Co.Ltd
Landscape design | Sasaki Associates
Structural system | Reinforced-concrete shear wall and steel truss folded plate roof
Main materials | Cold-gray titanium-zinc roof, concrete textural paint, dark-gray aluminum plate, wooden textural aluminum window frame, low-iron insulated low-E glass with built-in louvers, and oak composite floor

We designed a series of public facilities in Xuhui Runway Park, which was renovated from the century-old Longhua Airport located at the West Bund of Shanghai's Huangpu River. The activity homes—the most concentrated part of the series—showcase a stretch of three buildings set side-by-side that house a community pavilion, a coffee shop, and a restaurant.

Mapping the layout according to the runway park's linear site, we set up a series of concrete walls that are of different lengths at various intervals. These walls divide the space and support a truss-made folded plate roof system. The pitched roofs present a visual metaphor of airplanes taking off, as they extend in fluctuating heights through the runway park.

The walls and roofs define a series of internal spaces that are parallel to the runway and connected with each other, giving a passing nod to the "grouped houses" concept. This spatial ambiguity between openness and enclosure offers the facility the freedom to accommodate added functions in the future, thereby increasing the possibility to support a variety of uses.

All three buildings have been built based on this structural system; varying wall spacing, roof widths, and roof heights provide spaces in diverse scales. Natural light enters through high windows set in between the interlaced folded plates and creates varying atmospheres in the three buildings through a lively play of light and shadow. By organizing the system to be flexible, we were able to accord different characters to each building. The adaptive potential of the system is apparent through the semi-open space in the coffee shop, the courtyard in the community pavilion, and the loft and recess in the restaurant.

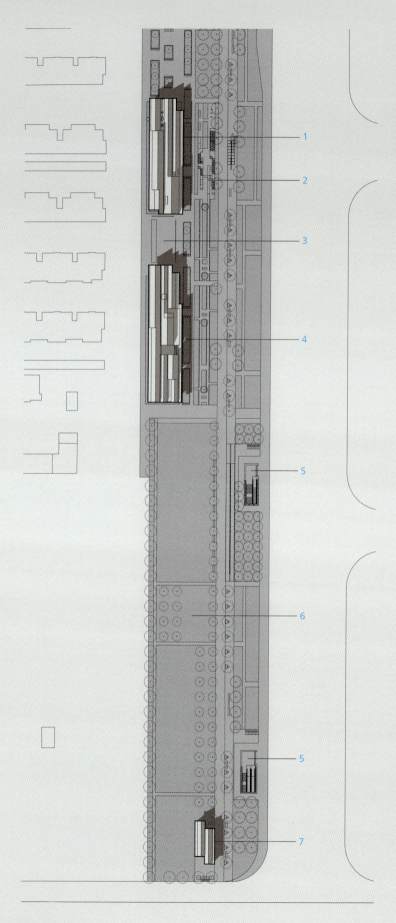

1	Restaurant
2	Playground
3	Fountain plaza
4	Community pavilion
5	Metro station
6	Event plaza
7	Coffee shop

Master plan

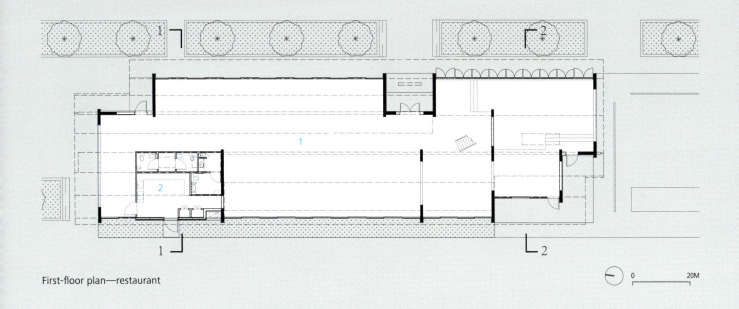

First-floor plan—restaurant

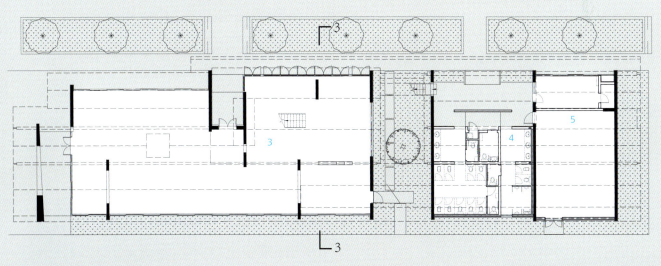

First-floor plan—community pavilion

1 Restaurant
2 Kitchen
3 Community pavilion
4 Restroom
5 Equipment room
6 Coffee shop

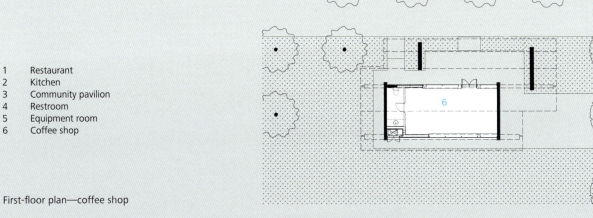

First-floor plan—coffee shop

203

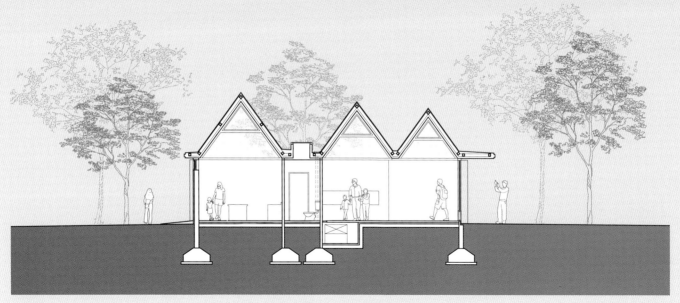
Section 1-1

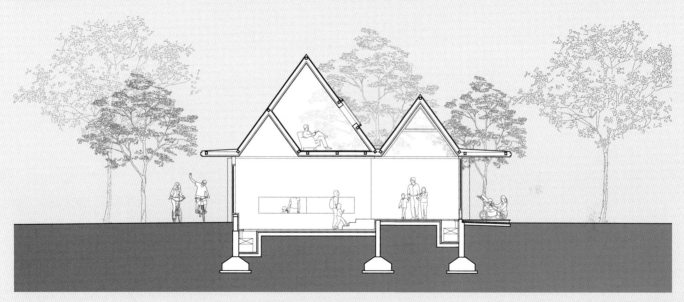
Section 2-2

Section 3-3

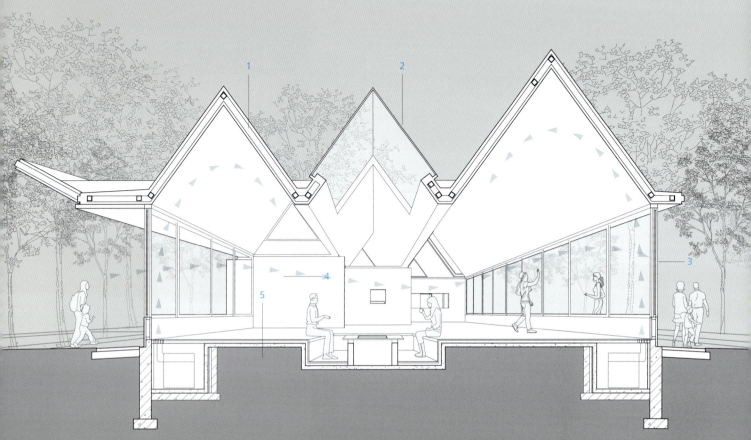

1   0.7 mm dark-gray titanium-zinc sheet
    6.0 mm ventilation and noise reduction mesh
    2.0 mm APP modified self-adhesive polyester waterproof bituminous membrane
    0.8 mm galvanized steel sheet leveling blanket
    0.6 mm 750-type profiled steel sheet
    120 mm mineral wool insulation layer (wrapped by mesh, within steel truss)
    Steel truss

2   Ceramic fritted low-iron insulated low-E glass

3   Low-iron insulated low-E glass with built-in louvers

4   Concrete textural paint
    Water-based waterproof primer
    Elastic primer, flexible water-resistant putty
    Second layer mortar and alkali-resistant coated mesh cloth and third layer adhesive mortar coat
    Anchor bolts
    First layer mortar and alkali-resistant coated mesh cloth
    50 mm rock wool insulation
    Adhesive binder
    12 mm WP15 pre-mixed mortar screed (with wire mesh sandwiched)
    200 mm reinforced-concrete shear wall

5   Two layers of wood floor paint
    25 mm hardwood flooring (back brushed with sodium fluoride preservative)
    50x50 mm main wood keel @400 with hollow of 20 mm, brushed with preservative
    80 mm C15 concrete subbase
    Packed soil

0   1M

Structure = supporting element + spatial definition + scene frames + historical echo

The flexibly arranged shear walls serve as both structural and spatial elements. The carefully placed openings on the walls allow visual connections between different spaces. The folded plate structure is realized by the steel truss; the cantilevered trusses balance the horizontal force and create the gray space under the eaves.

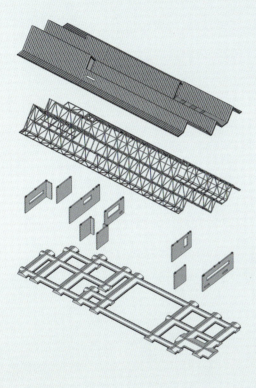

Soft light and breeze

Soft daylight enters through louvered windows on the east and west façades, as well as the high translucent ceramic fritted glass windows between the walls and roofs. These windows also circulate fresh air, complementing the under-floor air-conditioning system.

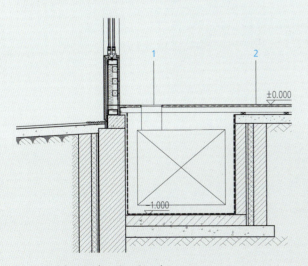

1   Stainless-steel grating air outlet
2   Composite wood floor

207

Extending along the linear layout of Xuhui Runway Park, the activity homes attract citizens of all ages and enhance community vitality.

The series of internal home-like spaces are parallel to the runway and connected with each other, giving a passing nod to the "grouped houses" concept.

221

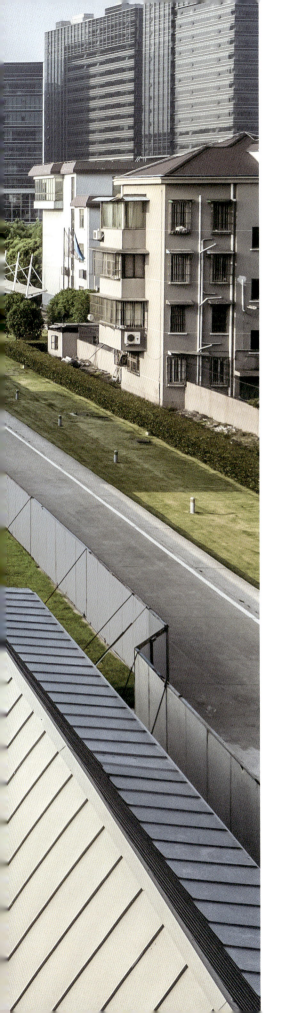

The pitched roofs fluctuate in varying heights and extend along the length of the runway park, presenting a visual metaphor of airplanes taking off.

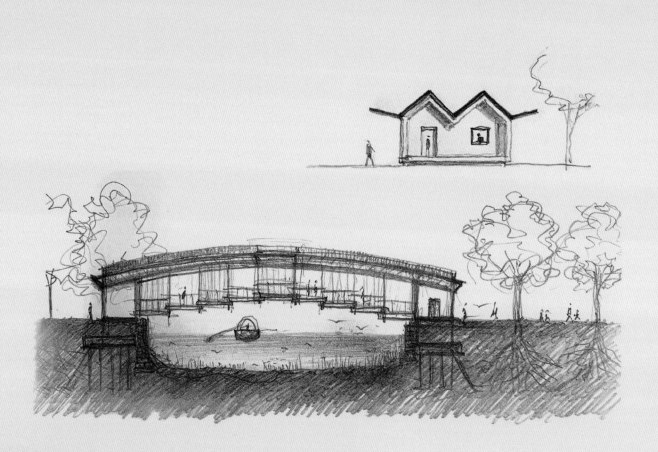

 Bridge of Nine Terraces

Rainbow Hung from Cornice

Location | Expo Village of the 11th Horticultural Exposition of Jiangsu Province, Nanjing, Jiangsu Province, China
Program | Pedestrian bridge
Site area | 1,292 ft² (120 m²)
Gross floor area | 3,229 ft² (400 m²)
Designed/built | 2018/2021
Design team | Zhu Xiaofeng, Zhou Yan
Client | Jiangsu Horticultural Exposition Construction and Development Co., Ltd
Structural consultant | Zhang Zhun (AND Office)
Local design institute | T. Y. Lin International Group
Structural system | Steel truss folded plate arch and concrete shear wall
Main materials | Titanium-zinc sheet roofing, timber, carbon steel pole, bamboo curtain, plastic-wood composite flooring, and cast-in-situ fair-faced concrete (small wood panel surface and washed pebble surface)

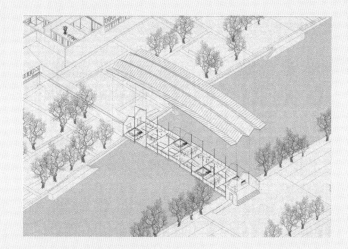

The Expo Village of the 11th Horticultural Exposition of Jiangsu Province is located along the northern slope of Xian Mountain. The northern part of the Expo Village faces Qixiang River and the Expo Treasure Museum located across the river. A covered bridge that spans 118 feet (36 meters) over the river functions as the northern pedestrian entryway into the Expo Village.

The bridge not only makes access convenient, but also serves as a place for visitors to gather, rest, and socialize. Due to the height difference between the revetment and the water level, the bridge needed to be raised in the middle. Based on these design conditions, the 26-foot-wide (8-meter-wide) bridge deck is divided into nine 13-by-26-foot (4-by-8-meter) platforms—like nine connected pavilions that gradually rise and fall. The most suited structural form for this concept was to use the pitched roofs of the bridge cover as the main structural arch to suspend the nine platforms. Through the joint efforts of the architects and structural engineers, steel trusses—arranged along the double gable roof—form a folded plate arch, which transforms the vertical load of the suspended platforms into internal forces that are transferred to the two ends of the arch structure.

Gravity and lateral thrust are loaded off onto the foundation on the revetment through the U-shaped concrete bridgehead. The nine suspended platforms are light and permeable, connected by ramps and steps, and provide areas for rest and to set up expo/market counters. The bridge heads, composed of shear walls on both sides, are simple and solid; the double gable roofs are extended to cover the bridge's shear wall, turning the bridgehead into two semi-outdoor cabins, presenting the pedestrian bridge with an implied meaning of returning home.

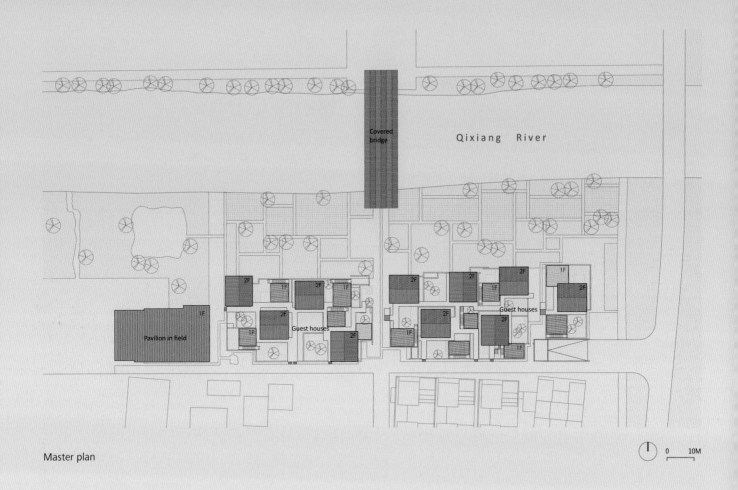

Master plan

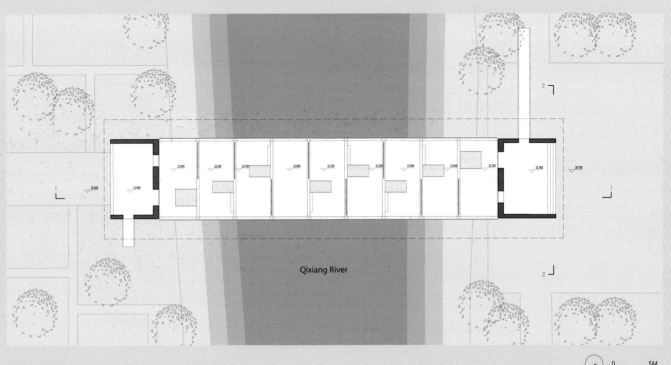

First-floor plan

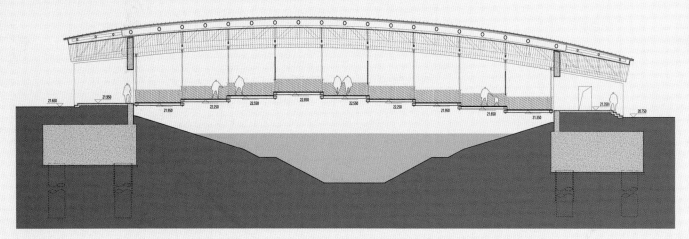

Section 1-1

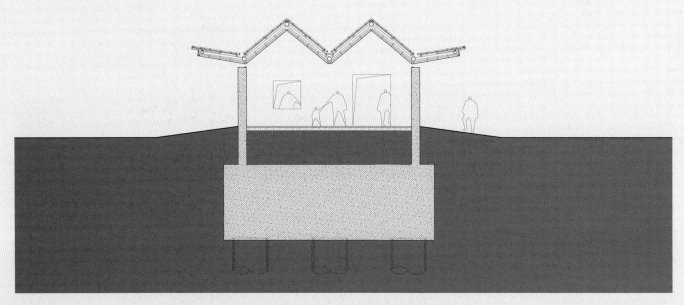

Section 2-2

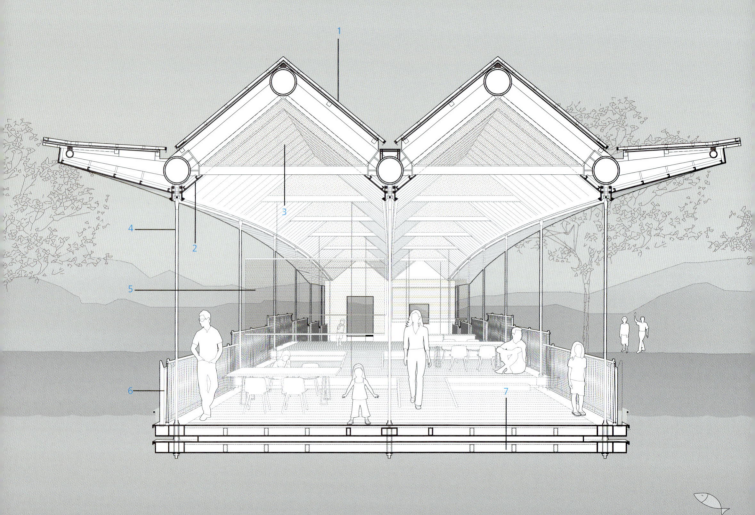

1	0.8-mm-thick titanium-zinc T50 vertical seaming plate 6 mm ventilation and noise reduction screen 1.2-mm-thick self-adhesive waterproof membrane 1-mm-thick galvanized leveling steel plate 0.6-mm-thick galvanized profiled steel sheet Rectangular tube keel 80×80×3 mm	4	White sling, anti-rust
		5	Decorative bamboo curtain
		6	Φ 8 mm black titanium 316 stainless-steel rod
2	CLT spruce high-grade solid wood board	7	40×125 mm bamboo floor with a gap of 4 mm Steel structure bridge deck with white fluorocarbon coating
3	White stainless-steel metal mesh		

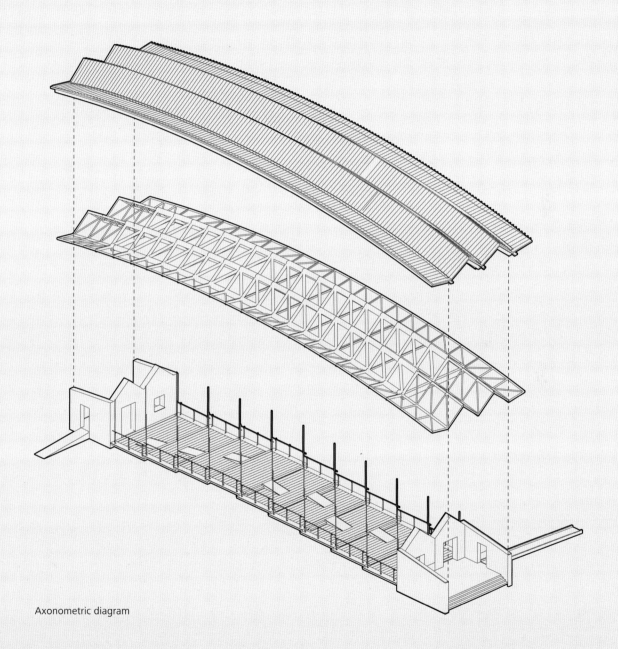

Axonometric diagram

229

Dual-purpose cornice

The cantilevered cornice formed by the tapered truss of the roof serves not only as the sunshade, but also as a strengthened edge to help balance the side thrust of the folded truss plate.

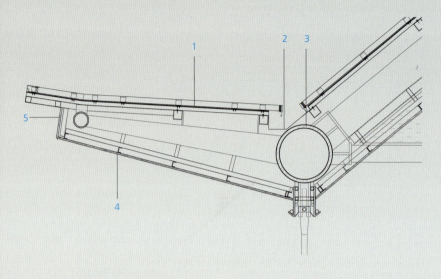

1   Cyan-gray titanium-zinc plate
2   Stainless-steel gutter
3   Lower chord tube ø 500 mm
4   Timber ceiling
5   Verge board

Stepping handrailing

A plan deflection of the railing avoids conflicts between the top rail and cables at the platform junction.

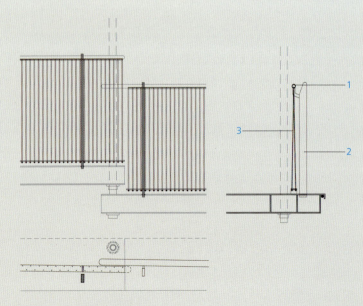

1   80×25 mm black titanium 316 stainless-steel column
2   40×3 mm black titanium 316 stainless-steel handrails
3   Φ 8 mm black titanium 316 stainless-steel rod

The busy lower chord

The lower chord at the bottom of the combined pitched truss works as a hub for all forces; it hangs the platforms by suspension rods, connects the horizontal tension chords, and supports the gutter.

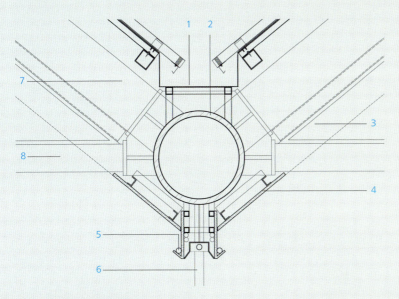

1 Stainless-steel gutter
2 Lower chord tube ø 500 mm
3 Timber fin grille
4 Timber ceiling
5 LED lighting fixture
6 Suspension rod
7 Diagonal web member
8 Horizontal tension chord

Penetrating rod

The suspension rod penetrates the edge beams of the stepping platforms with drivepipes to hold them tightly.

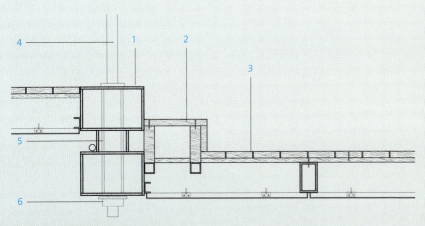

1 300×200 mm square steel tube
2 Wooden step
3 Wooden plank flooring
4 Suspender rod
5 Drivepipe ø 100 mm
6 Fastening bolt

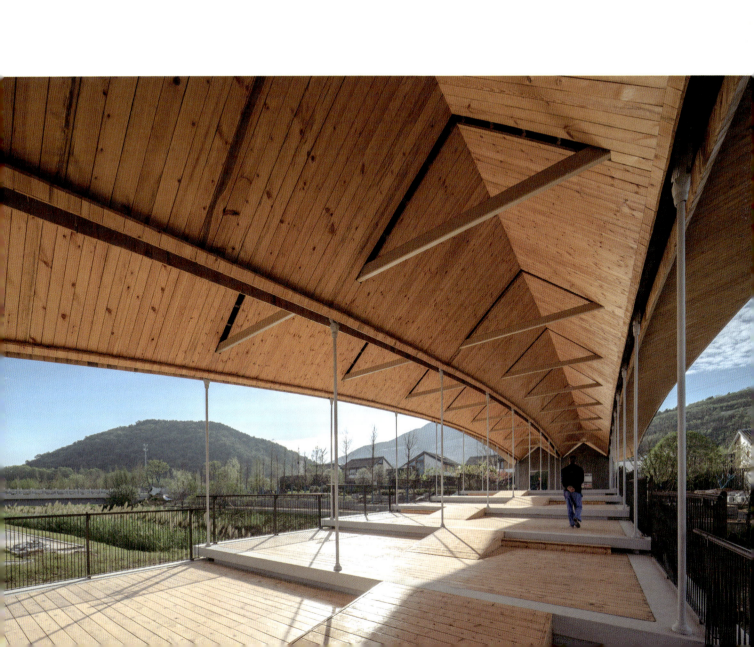

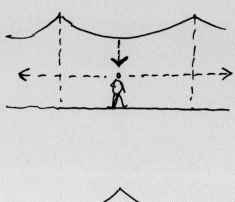

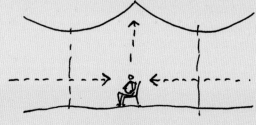

Dongyuan Qianxun Community Center

Interwoven Auras

Location | Xiangcheng District, Suzhou City, Jiangsu Province, China
Program | Community services
Site area | 45,822 ft² (4,257 m²)
Gross floor area | 35,812 ft² (3,327 m²)
Designed/built | 2016/2017
Project team | Zhu Xiaofeng, Zhuang Xinjia, Sheng Tai, Shi Yin, Du Shigang, Li Cheng, Fu Rong, Luo Qi, Xiao Zaiyuan, Shang Yunpeng
Client | Dongyuan Real Estate Development Group Co. Ltd
Structural consultant | Zhang Zhun (AND Office)
Local design institute | Suzhou Architectural Design & Research Institute Ltd
Landscape design | HWA Design Group
Structural system | Stacking walls as deep beams, steel truss, and inverted reinforced-concrete barrel shell roof
Main materials | Fair-faced concrete, aluminum-magnesium-manganese roofing system, and low-iron laminated thermal low-E glass

The community center is located in Suzhou, a canal city in southern Yangtze River Delta that boasts historical gardens and charming courtyard architectures. To the south side of the community center lies a wetland, through which a river meanders, charting its course from east to west. Assisted along by reeds and trees on the riverbanks, it flows on to greet the south side of the community center. The thriving nature in the area and the location's cultural heritage inspired the design concept of the project.

As a community center, the building needed to house facilities that could host community activities and provide public services for residents and the public. These included cultural festivals, social gatherings, art exhibitions, parent-child activities, sports events, and other community-based activities. These main functions shaped the internal requirements of the center. We strove to create a new spatial order that would effectively respond to both the community center's functional demands, as well as the external environment. In so doing, the community center would emerge as a dynamic activity space that realizes the coexistence of socialness and naturalness, and cohesion and openness.

After in-depth research on structural systems and spatial order, we decided to use a system of "stacked walls as deep beams" to construct the space. The walls provide enclosure and divide spaces, while the void provides openness and links spaces—it is the dual effort of this order that achieves the coexistence of cohesion and openness.

Inverted reinforced-concrete barrel shell roofs create an impression of being under waves: standing under the ridge, one gets a sense of stability similar to that of traditional gable roofs; standing under the valley, one experiences a dynamism that mimics rising tides. The interior impressions and the external appearance of the wavy gable walls express a connection with water and tie back to the traditional architectural style of southeast Yangtze River Delta. The alternately arranged walls and openings in this form-type merge architecture and nature to form a permeable courtyard cluster. Uniquely defined by stacked walls, the spaces cast interwoven auras created by the flow of light and the passing of time.

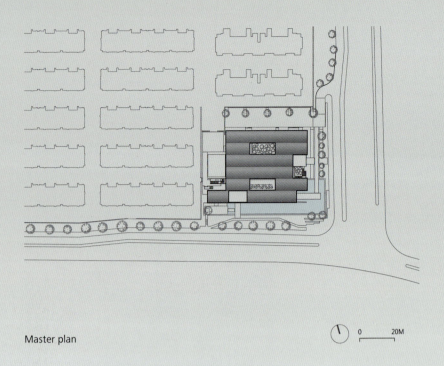

Master plan

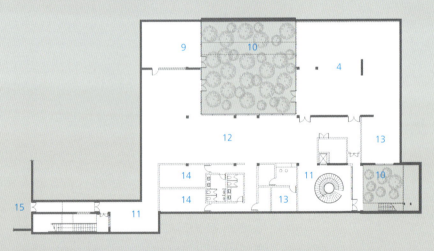

Lower-first-floor plan

1	Parent-child activities room	9	Yoga room
2	Lounge	10	Courtyard
3	Community center	11	Entrance hall
4	Art exhibition area	12	Fitness center
5	Convenience store	13	Office
6	Library	14	Locker room
7	Community workshop	15	Garage
8	Café		

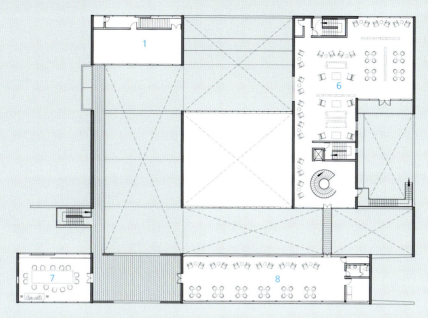
Second-floor plan

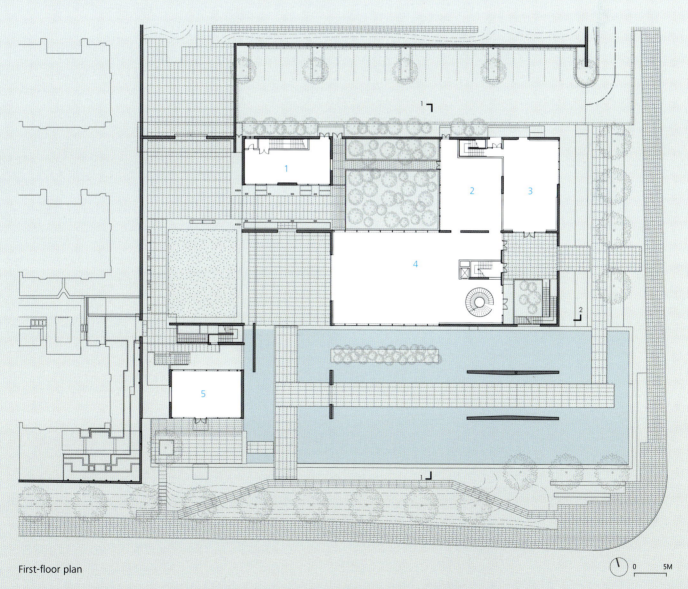
First-floor plan

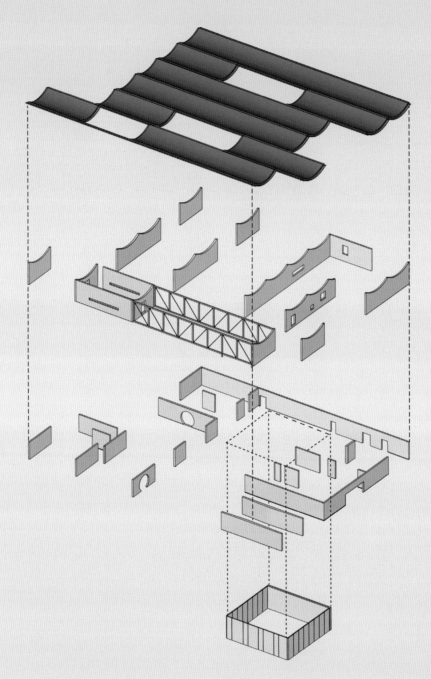
Axonometric diagram

Section 1-1

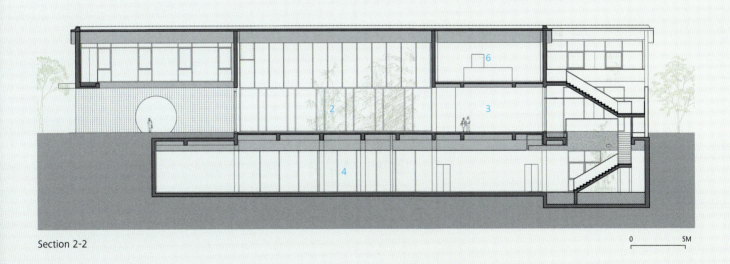

Section 2-2

1 Café
2 Courtyard
3 Art exhibition area
4 Fitness center
5 Locker room
6 Library

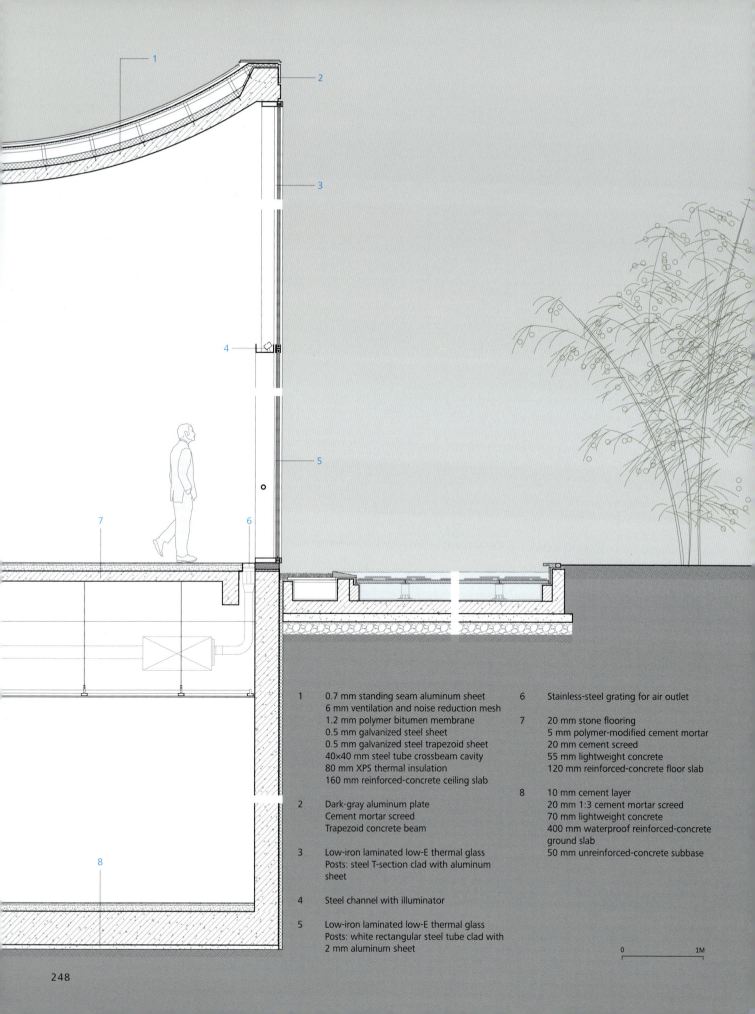

1   0.7 mm standing seam aluminum sheet
    6 mm ventilation and noise reduction mesh
    1.2 mm polymer bitumen membrane
    0.5 mm galvanized steel sheet
    0.5 mm galvanized steel trapezoid sheet
    40×40 mm steel tube crossbeam cavity
    80 mm XPS thermal insulation
    160 mm reinforced-concrete ceiling slab

2   Dark-gray aluminum plate
    Cement mortar screed
    Trapezoid concrete beam

3   Low-iron laminated low-E thermal glass
    Posts: steel T-section clad with aluminum sheet

4   Steel channel with illuminator

5   Low-iron laminated low-E thermal glass
    Posts: white rectangular steel tube clad with 2 mm aluminum sheet

6   Stainless-steel grating for air outlet

7   20 mm stone flooring
    5 mm polymer-modified cement mortar
    20 mm cement screed
    55 mm lightweight concrete
    120 mm reinforced-concrete floor slab

8   10 mm cement layer
    20 mm 1:3 cement mortar screed
    70 mm lightweight concrete
    400 mm waterproof reinforced-concrete ground slab
    50 mm unreinforced-concrete subbase

The tectonics of the inversed concrete shell

Technical strategy combining precise processing and low-tech construction:

- Precisely shaped and processed curved steel pipes are supported by ordinary scaffolding
- The curved steel pipes are covered with 3.9-inch-wide (100-millimeter-wide) strip planks
- The 3.9-by-7.9-foot (1.2-by-2.4-meter) glulam concrete formworks fully cover the strip planks and are manually trodden down
- Steel bars are laid and bound
- Concrete is poured in situ
- Insulation and waterproof layer are constructed
- Keel and aluminum-magnesium-manganese roof are constructed

Organized free drainage at the bottom of inverted barrel shell

The gutter, set at the lowest point of the inverted barrel roof, needs to be 23.6 inches (600 millimeters) wide. However, this would undermine the image of the fifth façade. Therefore, we overhang the metal roof panel above the gutter to make a gap drainage that is only 3.9 inches (100 millimeters) wide. In the semi-outdoor spaces, rainwater is collected from the gutters into customized stainless-steel slots and dripped into the reflecting pool below.

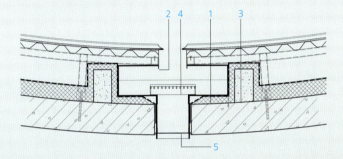

1 Concrete gutter
2 Flashing board
3 C20 fine stone concrete
4 Rain hopper
5 Metal grating

Texture of time on the white wall

The formwork for the shear walls was constructed by first nailing carbonized battens onto large smooth boards; 0.8-inch-wide (20-millimeter-wide) gaps were left between the battens so the concrete could overflow. Next, the formwork was removed to reveal a cladding-like paneled appearance with a wood grain texture impressed into the set concrete. Then, white paint was sprayed and workers used tuck-pointer trowels to scratch the concrete in a vertical direction to more distinctly reveal the wood grain texture left behind by the wooden formwork.

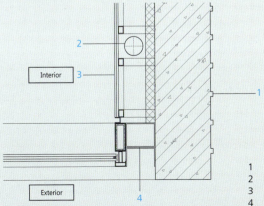

1 Extruded vertical stripes
2 Drainage pipe
3 Double-layered gypsum board
4 160×100 mm notch

249

The interior impressions and exterior look of the wavy gable walls express a connection with water and tie back to the traditional architectural style of southeast Yangtze River Delta.

The walls provide enclosure and divide spaces, while the void provides openness and links spaces—the dual character of this concept achieves the coexistence of cohesion and openness.

Uniquely defined by alternately stacked walls, the spaces merge architecture and nature to cast an interwoven aura created by the flow of light and the passing of time.

Deep Dive Rowing Club

Collaborating with Nature

Location | Century Park, Pudong New District, Shanghai, China
Program | Rowing training facilities and activities compound for youth
Site area | 1,292 ft^2 (120 m^2)
Gross floor area | 3,229 ft^2 (300 m^2)
Designed/built | 2016/2017
Design team | Zhu Xiaofeng, Li Qitong (project manager), Du Jie (project architect), Zhou Yan
Client | Vanke Education Group
Structural consultant | Zhang Zhun (AND Office)
Structural system | Steel framework
Main materials | Bangkirai plank, titanium-zinc sheet roofing, foldable thermal aluminum profile window system, white aluminum panel, composite timber panel, anti-rust paint, fluorocarbon coating, and plastic-wood composite flooring

Located at a river bend in Shanghai Century Park, the club is a rowing training center catered to youths. The site is home to a dense metasequoia forest, and in order to minimize the impact on the natural environment, we divided the program into four parts: the pier located at the southern river bend, the activity room set on the river, the changing room constructed on the old pier foundation, and the boat shed—the only part that occupies a small zone in the forest.

The changing room, a narrow volume covered by bangkirai panels, is more enclosed than other areas. This caters to the need for privacy in a changing area, while also doubling as an interval in the spatial experiences of the forest and the river.

The activity room on the river resembles a waterfront pavilion and presents the impression of an unmoored boat; its bottom is barge-like, with a rectangular steel grating that sits on pipe piles, and its cover is a 215.2-foot-long (20-meter-long) roof that is supported only by a pair of steel H-pillars at both ends. This grants the space a sense of freedom and openness. On the façade facing the river, absolute vastness is realized through three sets of foldable sliding windows, allowing a visual connection between indoor ergometer training and outdoor rowing training. Under the windows, a long, wide wooden sill provides seating that is complemented with a breathtaking view, making the space ideal for resting, chatting, or simply just enjoying the scenery.

The activity room is constructed slightly lower than the riverbank to give the space a cabin-like identity. Being in this space allows one to feel calm and connected to nature.

Covered with a plastic-wood floor and supported by clusters of buoys tied together, the pier connects to the shore through a ramp and a small ladder, both of which are linked by hinges so that they can be adjusted to the fluctuating water level of the river.

To avoid major felling or transplanting of the metasequoia forest, the boat huts are designed as three narrow pole sheds scattered in the forest. Their narrow form enables them to be constructed between the trees, and each is supported by tree-like columns and is open all around, with only a steel canopy. This transforms the retrieval and returning of boats into a relaxing and refreshing walk in the forest. Walking routes are also thoughtfully designed: translucent paths made of elevated stainless-steel grating are non-intrusive and permit insect and small animal activity, as well as vegetation to grow.

Through the design strategy of minimized and dispersed intervention, we realized this eco-friendly cluster in collaboration with nature. By expressing a cohesive relationship between architecture and environment, this project convincingly transmits the idea of sustainable construction.

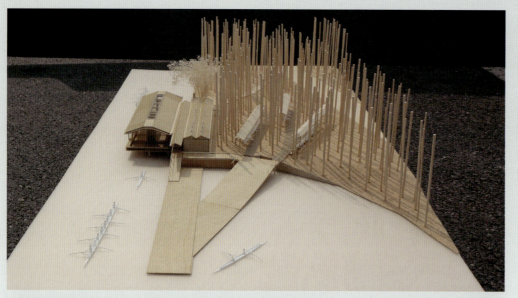

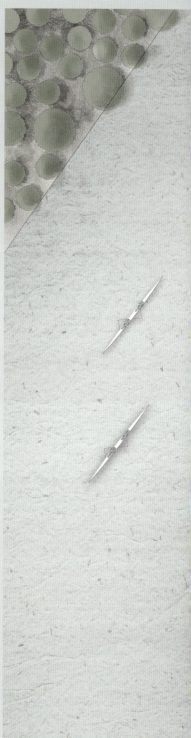

First-floor plan

266

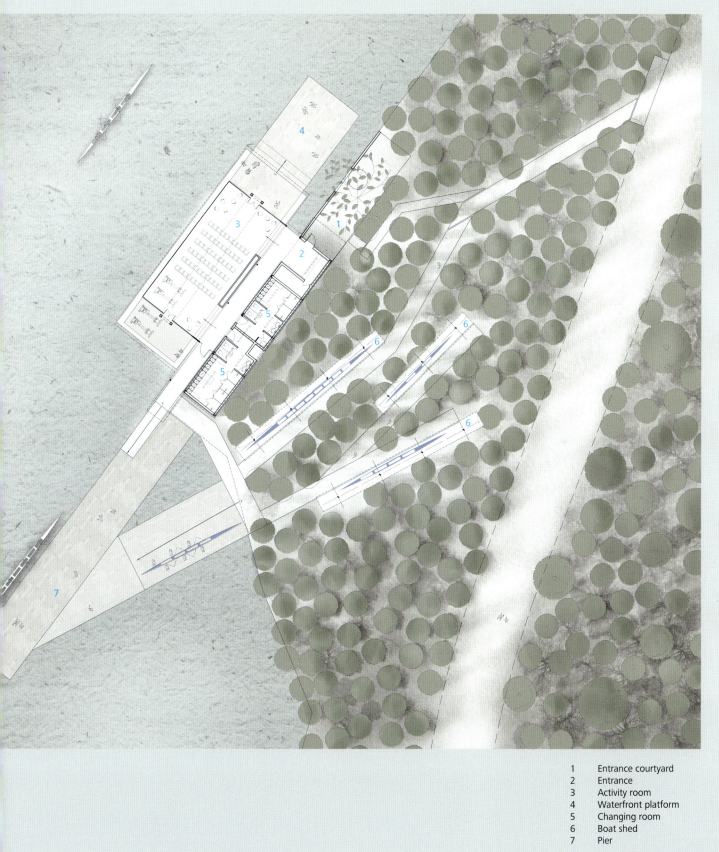

1	Entrance courtyard
2	Entrance
3	Activity room
4	Waterfront platform
5	Changing room
6	Boat shed
7	Pier

Section 0 1M

269

1	1.5 mm stainless-steel gutter with ø 40 mm stainless-steel outlet
2	0.7 mm titanium-zinc sheet Standing seam keel for titanium-zinc sheet 6 mm ventilation and noise reduction mesh 1.5 mm viscous polymer waterproof membrane 20 mm blockboard Polypropylene waterproof breathable membrane 50 mm keel filled with foam glass insulation board Polymer modified asphalt vapor barrier Steel beam Aluminum gusset plate ceiling with special keel and edge
3	Ceramic fritted tempered and laminated low-E insulated glass Steel beam Lightweight steel keel @1,200 Translucent membrane
4	0.7 mm titanium-zinc sheet Standing seam keel for titanium-zinc sheet 6 mm ventilation and noise reduction network 1.5 mm viscous polymeric waterproof membrane 20 mm blockboard Polypropylene waterproof breathable membrane 60 mm foam glass insulation board Polymer modified asphalt vapor barrier Steel beam
5	15 mm high-quality anticorrosive wood 40x40 mm timber keel @400, coated with preservative and fire protection paint 6 mm crack-resistant mortar with alkali-resistant mesh and thermal nail Keel with 40 mm mineral wool in between wrapped by vapor barrier 20 mm 1:3 cement mortar screed Polymer cement paste (with structural glue) Concrete brick wall
6	PVC waterproof membrane with weld processing 2 mm putty screed Polymer cement-based waterproof coating 1:3 thermal mortar sloping with minimal thickness of 20 mm Cement paste (with structural glue) 40 mm fine-aggregate concrete

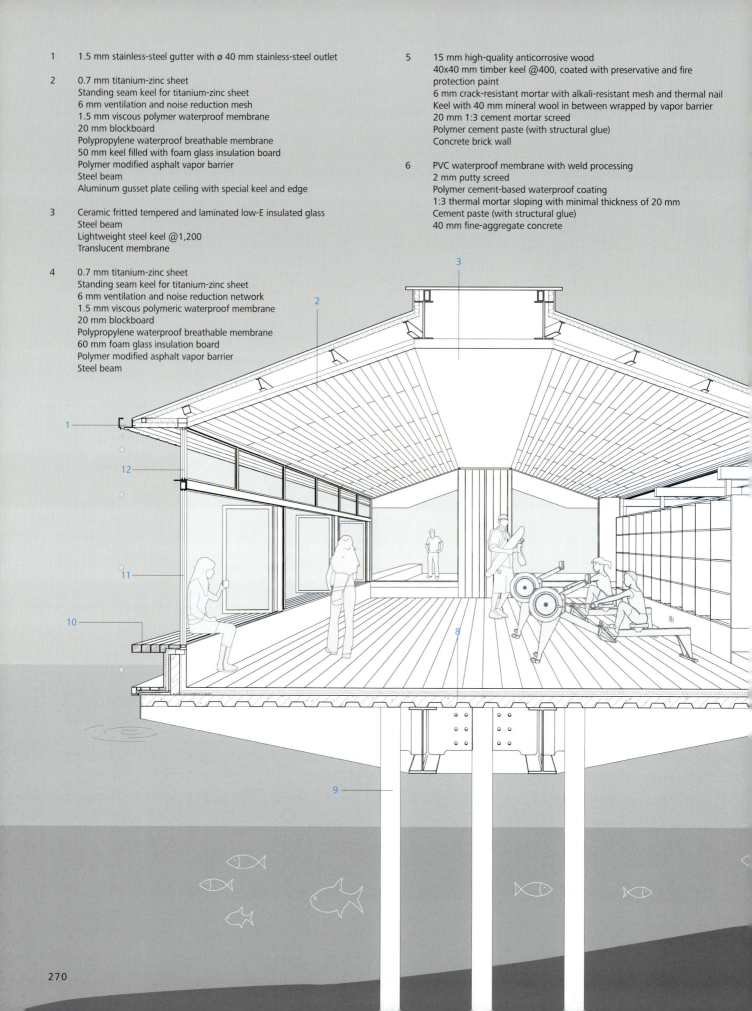

7 Checkered steel plate with 0.2 mm polyurethane paint
20 mm hardwood flooring, with sodium fluoride preservative and fire protection paint
40x40 mm timber keel @400, coated with preservative and fire protection paint, and filled with mineral wool in between
20 mm 1:3 cement mortar screed
40 mm fine stone concrete
Checkered steel plate

8 0.2 mm polyurethane paint
20 mm hardwood flooring, with sodium fluoride preservative and fire protection paint
40x40 mm timber keel @400, coated with preservative and fire protection paint, and filled with mineral wool in between
20 mm 1:3 cement mortar screed
Cement paste (with construction adhesive)
Profiled steel sheet and reinforced-concrete composite slab

9 Steel pipe pile

10 Exterior seat: 100x80 mm bangkirai plank

11 Foldable sliding casements: tempered low-E insulated glass with white fluorocarbon-coated window frame

12 Fixed high windows: tempered low-E insulated glass

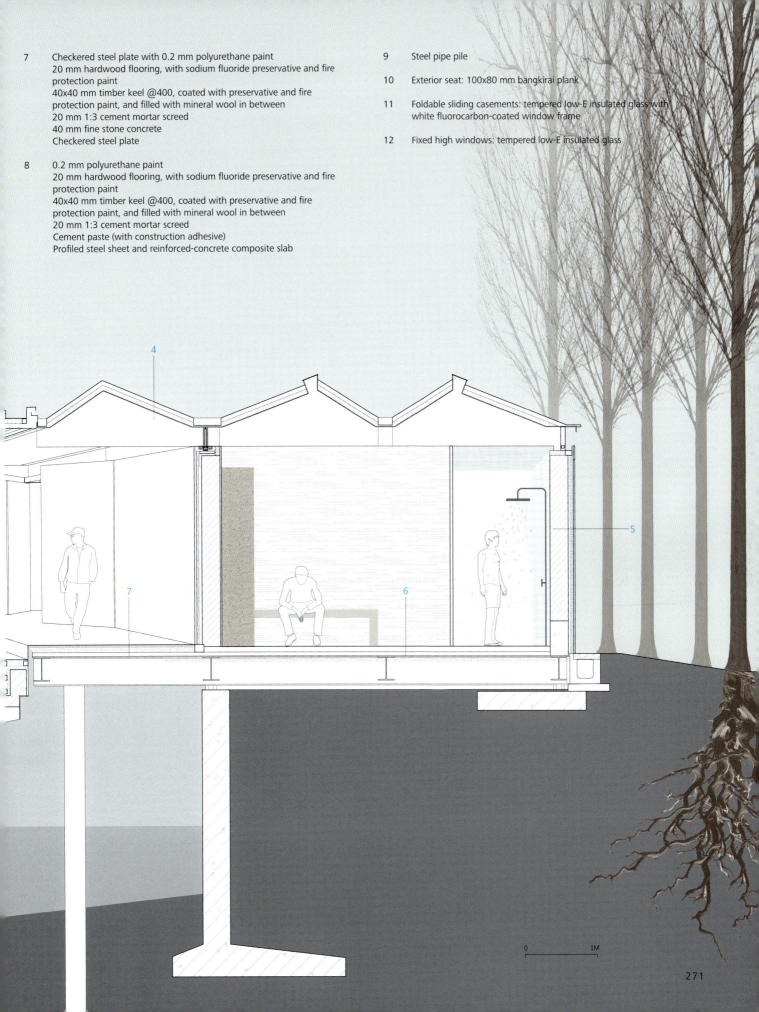

Accesses for people and light: door between columns and skylight between beams

The activity room is covered by a 65.6-foot-long (20-meter-long) double-pitch roof. The roof is supported only by a pair of steel H-pillars at either end, awarding the space an energizing open feel. The H-pillars cleverly frame the doors leading to the exterior platforms and support dual beams that inlay a skylight in between. Perceived as a whole, the H-pillars on the central axis and the suspended eaves on either side reflect a visual metaphor of a rower rowing a boat.

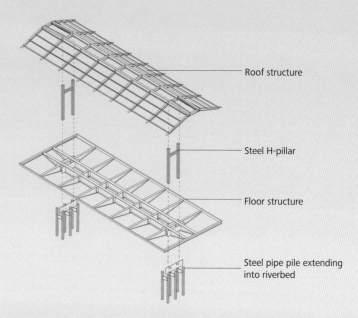

Roof structure

Steel H-pillar

Floor structure

Steel pipe pile extending into riverbed

The adaptation of folded plate

The roof of the changing room is made of folded steel plates supported by gable-shaped beams. It overhangs at both ends forming the entrance canopies, which are strengthened and stabilized by steel bars at the lower part. The linear skylight and high windows bring natural light in and ventilate the locker and shower area.

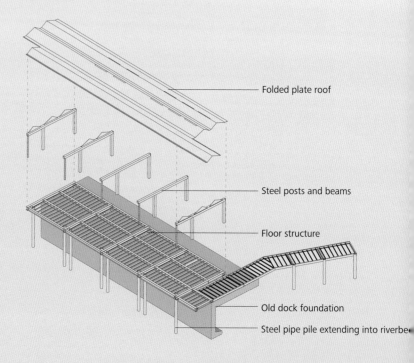

Folded plate roof

Steel posts and beams

Floor structure

Old dock foundation

Steel pipe pile extending into riverbed

Thin sheds for boats

In the metasequoia forest, three 5.2-foot-wide (1.6-meter-wide) and 42.7- to 59-foot-long (13- to 18-meter-long) sheds house the boats. In each coupled column, four pairs of bolts fasten a pair of steel angles and four horizontally suspended rods together. The suspended rods serve as mounts and support the weight of the boats alongside the pair of steel angle columns, which bifurcate at the top to support the double-pitched aluminum canopy.

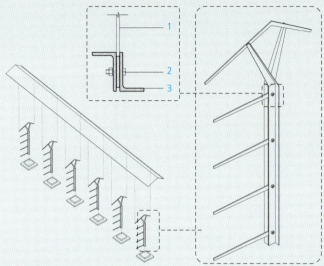

1   Suspended rods to support boats
2   High-strength bolts
3   Steel angle

Eco-friendly pathway

For pathways, we trailed 600 small concrete blocks as the foundation for stainless-steel grills that are placed on top. These permeable paths allow both flora and fauna in the area to exist and thrive.

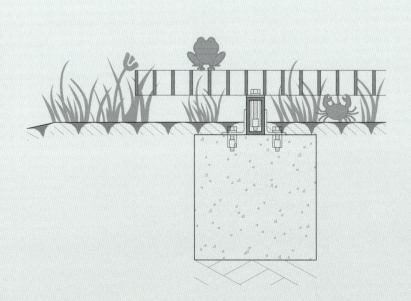

273

Both architecture and boat are an extension of the human body–mind. The mutual definition between structure and space, just like the one between mechanism and boat, embodies the wisdom of rowing—a cohesive integration of humans and their extension.

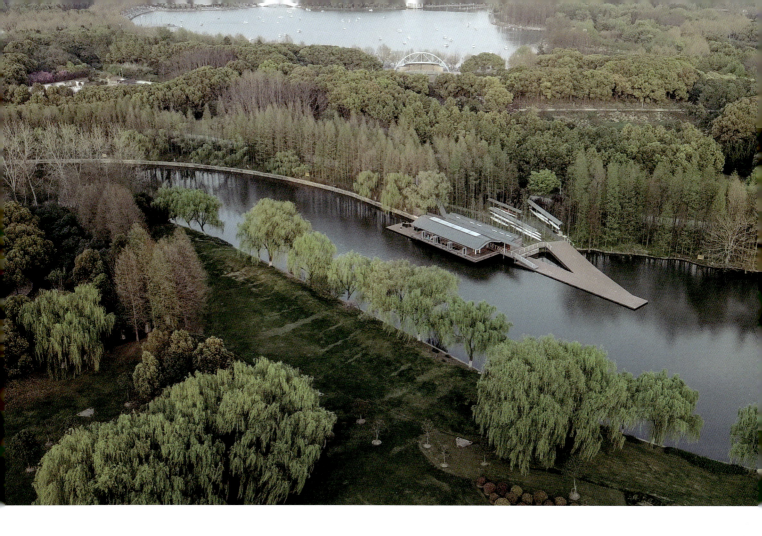

The activity room on the river appears like an unmoored boat surrounded by nature.

APPENDIX

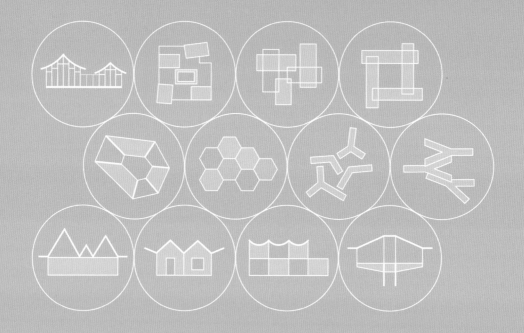

gpu New Town Grand Community Middle School

on | Qingpu District, Shanghai, China
am | Secondary school
floor area | 183,309.4 ft² (17,030 m²)
ned/built | 2011 (concept)
team | Zhu Xiaofeng, Zhuang Xinjia, Li Shuo, Su Shengliang
| Shanghai Dianshanhu New Town Development Ltd

Shanghai Liu Haisu Art Museum

Location | Changning District, Shanghai, China
Program | Art museum
Gross floor area | 134,355.1 ft² (12,482 m²)
Designed/built | 2012 (competition bid)
Design team | Zhu Xiaofeng, Li Qitong, Zhou Wei, Liang Shan, Su Shengliang, Wu Jian, Xu Xiwen
Client | Liu Haisu Art Museum

Dianshanhu Sanfendang Waterfront Area Urban Design

Location | Qingpu District, Shanghai, China
Program | Resort, hotel, housing, and public facilities
Site Area | 5,288,309.2 ft² (491,300 m²)
Gross floor area | 1,181,900 ft² (109,900 m²)
Designed/built | 2012 (concept)
Design team | Zhu Xiaofeng, Li Qitong, Liang Shan, Su Shengliang
Client | Qingpu District Urban Planning Bureau

w Town Grand Community Grocery

gpu District, Shanghai, China
cery store
a | 33,884.8 ft² (3,148 m²)
| 2011 (concept)
Zhu Xiaofeng, Xu Xiwen
ai Dianshanhu New Town Development Ltd

Longfor Yangzhou Showroom

Location | Yangzhou, Jiangsu Province, China
Program | Marketing center
Gross floor area | 10,763.9 ft² (1,000 m²)
Designed/built | 2012 (concept)
Design team | Zhu Xiaofeng, Zhuang Xinjia, Xu Xiwen
Client | Wuxi Longfor Real Estate Co. Ltd

Zijin (New Harbor) Technology and Entrepreneurship Neighborhood

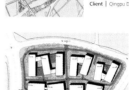

Location | Nanjing, Jiangsu Province, China
Program | Factory and offices
Gross floor area | 1,086,745.9 ft² (100,962 m²)
Designed/built | 2012/2014
Design team | Zhu Xiaofeng, Zhuang Xinjia, Hu Qiming
Client | Zijin (New Harbor) Technology and Entrepreneurship Neighborhood Development Co. Ltd

w Town Grand Community Kindergarten

gpu District, Shanghai, China
dergarten
a | 93,107.8 ft² (8,650 m²)
| 2011 (concept)
Zhu Xiaofeng, Ding Penghua
ai Dianshanhu New Town Development Ltd

Shanghai International Automobile Town Office Tower

Location | Jiading District, Shanghai, China
Program | Offices and public facilities
Gross floor area | 177,820 ft² (16,520 m²)
Designed/built | 2012 (concept)
Design team | Zhu Xiaofeng, Li Qitong, Su Shengliang
Client | Shanghai International Automobile City Group Co. Ltd

Vanke Hongqiao No. 11

Location | Minhang District, Shanghai, China
Program | Housing, retail services, and offices
Gross floor area | 1,911,670.5 ft² (17.76 ha)
Designed/built | 2012 (concept)
Design team | Zhu Xiaofeng, Ding Penghua, Cai Mian
Client | Vanke Group, Shanghai Branch

2012

Ecological Island

ngpu District, Shanghai, China
ousing and clubhouse
ea | 128,198.2 ft² (11,910 m²)
t | 2011 (concept)
Zhu Xiaofeng, Zhuang Xinjia, Cai Mian, Xu Xiwen
Money Information Co. Ltd

Suzhou Hanbi Academy

Location | Suzhou, Jiangsu Province, China
Program | Academic facilities
Gross floor area | 379,750.8 ft² (35,280 m²)
Designed/built | 2012/2019
Design team | Zhu Xiaofeng, Zhuang Xinjia, Li Qitong, Cai Mian, Liang Shan, Jiang Meng, Pablo Gonzalez Riera, Du Shigang, Su Wushun, Zhou Yan
Client | Suzhou Wuzhong District Government

Shanghai Google Creators' Society Center

Location | Xuhui District, Shanghai, China
Program | Exhibition center, science and culture center, and teahouse
Gross floor area | 7,857 ft² (730 m²)
Designed/built | 2012/2013
Design team | Zhu Xiaofeng, Ding Penghua, Cai Mian, Yang Hong
Client | China Fortune Properties

Taizhou Photovoltaics Apartments

Location | Taizhou, Jiangsu Province, China
Program | Housing
Gross floor area | 10,807 ft² (1,004 m²)
Designed/built | 2012 (schematic design)
Design team | Zhu Xiaofeng, Zhuang Xinjia, Wu Jian, Xu Xiwen, Ding Penghua, Jiang Meng
Client | Taizhou Chengxing Real Estate Ltd and Taizhou Chengxun Real Estate Ltd

Shenzhen Pingshan Cultural Community

Location | Shenzhen, Guangdong Province, China
Program | Cultural facilities and bookstore
Gross floor area | block A—587,709.5 ft² (54,600 m²)
                   block B—590,723.4 ft² (54,880 m²)
Designed/built | 2012 (concept)
Design team | Zhu Xiaofeng, Ding Penghua
Client | Pingshan District Government

anghai Sichuan Road

ngkou District, Shanghai, China
fices and retail facilities
ea | 1,046,833.3 ft² (97,254 m²)
t | 2011 (concept)
Zhu Xiaofeng, Li Wenjia
Shanghai

Bilingual Kindergarten Affiliated to East China Normal University

Location | Anting Town, Jiading District, Shanghai, China
Program | Kindergarten (with fifteen classes)
Gross floor area | 71,042 ft² (6,600 m²)
Designed/built | 2012/2015
Design team | Zhu Xiaofeng, Li Qitong, Ding Penghua, Yang Hong, Du Jie, Shi Yan'an, Cai Mian, Du Shigang, Jiang Meng, Hu Qiming, Guo Ying
Client | Shanghai International Automobile City Group Co. Ltd

Chongqing Zhonghang Boutique Hotel

Location | Chongqing, China
Program | Hotel
Gross floor area | 93,646 ft² (8,700 m²)
Designed/built | 2012 (schematic design)
Design team | Zhu Xiaofeng, Li Qitong, Jiang Meng, Hu Qiming
Client | Shenzheng Licheng Real Estate Consultant Ltd

Pao School Sports Complex
Location | Changning District, Shanghai, China
Program | Assembly hall, swimming pool, indoor activity space, multifunction gymnasium, special classrooms, library, and rooftop playground
Gross floor area | 86,703.3 ft² (8,055 m²)
Designed/built | 2019 (concept)
Design team | Zhu Xiaofeng, Zhuang Xinjia, Jiang Meng, Wang Junyuan, Shen Ziwei, Lin Xiaosheng, Sun Ying, Chen Yujin, Zeng Jing
Client | YK Pao School, Changning District Education Bureau

Huazhan Campus of Shanghai Gaoan Road No. 1 Primary School

Yangling Culture Center
Location | Chizhou City, Anhui Province, China
Program | Reception center, bookstore, children's classroom, and teahouse
Gross floor area | 6,243.1 ft² (580 m²)
Designed/built | 2020 (concept)
Design team | Zhu Xiaofeng, Li Qitong, Zhou Yan, Chen Xuanxiang, Geng Yutong, Sun Jianong, Lin Ying
Client | Anhui Cuiming Valley Tourism Development Co., Ltd

Zhangrun Office Building

Suzhou Archives Center of Agricultural Bank of China
Location | Kunshan City, Jiangsu Province, China
Program | Archive facilities
Gross floor area | 260,766.5 ft² (24,226 m²)
Designed/built | 2019 (concept)
Design team | Zhu Xiaofeng, Li Qitong, Zhang Xuan, Wang Mingzhen
Client | Agricultural Bank of China

Longde Road Pedestrian Bridge Over Suzhou River
Location | Putuo District, Shanghai, China
Program | Bridge
Gross floor area | 13,562.5 ft² (1,260 m²)
Designed/built | 2021 (concept)
Design team | Zhu Xiaofeng, Li Qitong, Pi Liming, Song Yixuan, Su Kaiqiang, Geng Yutong, Huo Yanlong
Client | Putuo District Municipal Water Engineering and Construction Center

Active Renovation of Gu's Old in Qigan Village
Location | Pudong New District, Shanghai, China
Program | Residence, neighborhood activity center, workshop, and other community activities
Renovation scale | 28 bays of the old house
Designed/built | 2018 (concept)
Design team | Zhu Xiaofeng, Zhuang Xinjia, Du Jie, Chen Tianle, Wang Junyuan, Lin Xiaosheng, Filippa Wang, Zhang Han
Client | Pudong New District Zhoupu Town

Hunan Road Villa Renovation
Location | Xuhui District, Shanghai, China
Program | Office facilities
Gross floor area | 3,196.9 ft² (297 m²)
Designed/built | 2019 (concept)
Design team | Zhu Xiaofeng, Zhuang Xinjia, Zhou Yan, Song Yixuan, Sun Jianong, Li Jing
Client | Tianshun Holdings

East Xitang (Phase 2)

2020   2021

Collective Village in Laogang Town
Location | Pudong New District, Shanghai, China
Program | Housing and community facilities
Gross floor area | 513,201.7 ft² (47,678 m²)
Designed/built | 2019 (concept)
Design team | Zhu Xiaofeng, Zhuang Xinjia, Jiang Meng, Shen Ziwei, He Wenxing, Zhang Tianyu, Wang Minzheng, Zhou Yan
Client | Pudong New District Planning and Natural Resource Bureau

Jiaxing Three Towers Station
Location | Jiaxing City, Zhejiang Province, China
Program | Lounge, teahouse, restroom facilities, and electrical distribution room
Gross floor area | 6,243.1 ft² (580 m²)
Designed/built | 2020 (concept)
Design team | Zhu Xiaofeng, Li Qitong, Jiang Meng, Jiang Zaijie
Client | Shangjia Group

Pudong Adolescent Activity Center and Civic Art Center

Annexe in Butterfly Bay Green Park
Location | Jingan District, Shanghai, China
Program | Landscape gallery, restroom facilities, and electrical distribution room
Gross floor area | 1,722.2 ft² (160 m²)
Designed/built | 2020 (concept)
Design team | Zhu Xiaofeng, Li Qitong, Song Yixuan, Sun Jianong
Client | Jing'an District Construction and Management Commission

Intco Center

Flower Market at Qinzhou Road
Location | Xuhui District, Shanghai, China
Program | Flower market and workshops
Gross floor area | 129,166.9 ft² (12,000 m²)
Designed/built | 2019 (concept)
Design team | Zhu Xiaofeng, Li Qitong, Zhu Xiaoye, Chen Xiafei
Client | Xuhui Garden Development Co., Ltd.

Byte Dance Chengdu Office Building
Location | Chengdu, Sichuan Province, China
Program | Office
Gross floor area | 1,176,200 ft² (109,275 m²)
Designed/built | 2020 (concept)
Design team | Zhu Xiaofeng, Li Qitong, Zhu Xiaoye, Song Yixuan, Geng Yutong, Chen Xuanxiang, Sun Ying
Client | Beijing Byte Dance Technology Co., Ltd

Shenzhen Sands Bay Pavilion
Location | Shenzhen, China
Program | Pavilion
Gross floor area | 2,691 ft² (250 m²)
Designed/built | 2021 (concept)
Design team | Zhu Xiaofeng, Li Qitong, Chen Xuanxiang, Geng Yutong, Sun Jianong
Client | Kaisa Group Holdings Co. Ltd

Shenzhen Conservatory of Music
Location | Shenzhen, China
Program | Concert hall, teaching facilities, and dormitory
Gross floor area | 1,396,300 ft² (129,722 m²)
Designed/built | 2020 (concept)
Design team | Zhu Xiaofeng, Li Qitong, Zhu Xiaoye
Cooperator | Höweler + Yoon Architecture, LLP
Client | Engineering Design Management Center, Shenzhen Construction Department

Expo Village, 11th Horticultural Exposition of Jiangsu Province (features Bridge of Nine Terraces)

SCENIC ARCHITECTURE OFFICE

Scenic Architecture Office was founded in Shanghai in 2004. In any project we undertake, we usually start by determining the various needs of body–mind, nature, and society, and try to establish a balanced and dynamic relationship between these aspects through ontological orders composed by space, time, and tectonics. In our recent years of practice, we have been focusing on exploring the potential of settlement space and tectonic form-type in the present to carve a new identity for contemporary architecture niched between Chinese tradition and the future.

The works of Scenic Architecture Office have been widely published by both international and local media, and we have also been invited to participate in various international architectural exhibitions, including Shanghai Urban Space Art Season; China Contemporary at Netherlands Architecture Institute, Rotterdam; China Design Now at London's Victoria and Albert Museum; Contemporary Chinese Architecture at Cité de l'architecture et du Patrimoine; Architopia at CIVA, Brussels; Shenzhen Biennale; New Trends of Architecture in Europe and Asia-Pacific; Un-Natural at BCA; Venice Architecture Biennale; Chengdu Biennale; Hong Kong Biennale; Milano Triennial; China Design Grand Exhibition; Shanghai West Bund Biennale; Eastern Promises—Contemporary Architecture and Spatial Practice in East Asia; Zai Xing Tu Mu—Fifteen Chinese Architects Exhibition; and Towards a Critical Pragmatism: Contemporary Architecture in China.

Our work has received many accolades both at home and abroad, and has earned awards like the Far Eastern Architectural Design Award, China Architecture Award, Architizer A+ Award, UED Museum Design Award, WAACA Award, ASSC Architectural Design Award, and ArchDaily Annual China Architecture Award.

Zhu Xiaofeng

Zhu Xiaofeng, the founding principal of Scenic Architecture Office, is a chartered member of the Royal Institute of British Architects, a member of the Architectural Culture Academic Committee of the Architectural Society of China, and a member of the Academic Department of Shanghai Architectural Society. Zhu attained his master's degree from Harvard University Graduate School of Design and his doctorate's degree from Tongji University. Since 2012, he has been lecturing at Tongji University as a guest professor in the College of Architecture and Urban Planning.

Profession	2004–present	**Scenic Architecture Office, Shanghai** Founder, Design Principal
	1999–2004	**Kohn Pedersen Fox Associates (KPF), New York** Associate Principal
	1994–1997	**Shenzhen University Institute of Architectural Design, Shenzhen** Associate Architect
Education	2012–2020	**Tongji University** Doctorate of Philosophy in Architecture
	1997–1999	**Harvard University Graduate School of Design** Master of Architecture (post-professional degree)
	1989–1994	**Shenzhen University School of Architecture** Bachelor of Architecture (with distinction)
Teaching	2012–present	**Tongji University School of Architecture and Urban Planning** Guest Professor and Design Instructor
	2013	**Hong Kong University Faculty of Architecture** Shanghai Center Visiting Studio Instructor
	2004	**Shenzhen University School of Architecture** Theme Studio Instructor
	1998–1999	**Boston Architectural Center** A-1 Studio Instructor
	1996–1997	**Shenzhen University School of Architecture** Core Studio Instructor

DISTINCTIONS

2021

WAACA2020, City Regeneration Award
Excellence prize: Yunjin Road Activity Homes

WAACA2020, Design Experiment Award
Shortlist: Dongyuan Qianxun Community Center

2020

Architizer A+ Award
Finalist in Architecture + Concrete category: Dongyuan Qianxun Community Center

The 19th Excellent Engineering Design Award of Jiangsu Province
Second prize: Dongyuan Qianxun Community Center

2020 Yangtze River Delta Public Cultural Space Innovation Design Competition
100 Public Cultural Space Award Public Reading Space: Lattice Book House

2020 Yangtze River Delta Public Cultural Space Innovation Design Competition
100 Public Cultural Space Award Cross-border Cultural Space: Yunjin Road Activity House

2020 Yuanye Award
Architecture Silver Award: Zhangrun Tower

IDA 2020
Bronze Award: Yunjin Road Activity House

IDA 2020
Bronze Award: Dongyuan Qianxun Community Center

2019

WAACA2016, Design Experiment Award
Shortlist: Deep Dive Rowing Club

2018

ArchDaily 2018 China Architecture Annual Award
Third place: Dongyuan Qianxun Community Center

2017

The Seventh ASSC Architectural Design Award
Distinguished prize: Bilingual Kindergarten Affiliated to East China Normal University

IEED International Eco-design Award
Best Eco Architecture Design Award: Huaxin Business Center (Shanghai Google Creators' Society Center)

2016

WAACA2016, Design Experiment Award
Shortlist: Bilingual Kindergarten Affiliated to East China Normal University

2015

The Sixth ASSC Architectural Design Award
Excellence prize: Nanjing Zijin (New Port) Special Community Initiative Area for Hitech and Entrepreneurship

2014

Far Eastern Architectural Design Award
Excellence prize: Huaxin Business Center (Shanghai Google Creators' Society Center)

Architizer A+ Award
Jury winner in Office Building—Low-rise category: Huaxin Business Center (Shanghai Google Creators' Society Center)

Architizer A+ Award
Finalist in Museums category: Zhujiajiao Museum of Humanities and Arts

WAACA2014, WA Technological Innovation Award
Excellence prize: Huaxin Business Center (Shanghai Google Creators' Society Center)

WAACA2014, WA Design Experiment Award
Finalist: Huaxin Business Center (Shanghai Google Creators' Society Center)

2013

Shanghai Excellent Project Design Award
Second place: Zhujiajiao Museum of Humanities and Arts

2012

China Architecture Media Awards
Finalist in Young Architect category: Zhu Xiaofeng

WAACA 2012
Finalist: Zhujiajiao Museum of Humanities and Arts

2011

UED Museum Design Award
Winning prize: Zhujiajiao Museum of Humanities and Arts

	2009	Perspective 40 Under 40 Award (Leading Young Designers in Asia) Winner: Zhu Xiaofeng
	1999	Guangdong Province Excellent Project Design Award Second place: Shenzhen College Students' Activity Center

EXHIBITIONS

2021

The Rebirth of Form-Type, **Exhibition of Featured Works of Scenic Architecture Office,** Tongji University, Shanghai

17th Venice Biennale International Architecture Exhibition, **Dongyuan Qianxun Community Center,** Venice, Italy

Shanghai Urban Space Art Season, **Huazhan campus of Gaoan Road No. 1 Primary School,** Shanghai, China

2019

Unknown City, **Swarm City**, Shenzhen, China

Pingshan Art Museum Exibition, **Dongyuan Qianxun Community Center and other works**, Shenzhen, China

2018

China Design Exhibition, **Deep Dive Rowing Club**, Shenzhen, China

Vanke Art Exhibition, **Deep Dive Rowing Club**, Suzhou, China

16th Venice Biennale International Architecture Exhibition, **Tower Park**, Venice, Italy

2017

Shanghai Urban Space Art Season, **Huaxin Business Center (Shanghai Google Creators' Society Center)**, Shanghai, China

Bienal de Curitiba, **Lattice Book House and other works**, Curitiba, Brazil

Scenic Architecture Office—Lattice Boundary, **Lattice Book House and recent works**, Shanghai, China

Shanghai Urban Space Art Season Special Exhibition, **Pudong Adolescent Activity Center and Civic Art Center**, Shanghai, China

2016

Towards A Critical Pragmatism: Contemporary Architecture in China, **Huaxin Business Center (Shanghai Google Creators' Society Center)**, Harvard Graduate School of Design, Boston, United States

Aedes Zai Xing Tu Mu—Fifteen Chinese Architects Exhibition, Berlin, Germany

China Design Exhibition, **Huaxin Business Center (Shanghai Google Creators' Society Center)**, Shenzhen, China

2015

Shanghai Urban Space Art Season: China Fortune Urban Revitalization Practice Exhibition, **Huaxin Business Center (Shanghai Google Creators' Society Center)**, Shanghai, China

Beijing Design Week: 10x100—UED 100 Architects During 10 Years, **Huaxin Business Center (Shanghai Google Creators' Society Center)**, Beijing, China

Beijing Design Week: 1,000 Architectures in China (2000–2015), **Lattice Book House and other works**, Beijing, China

Shanghai Urban Space Art Season: West Bund Biennial Exhibition, **Shengli Street Neighborhood Committee and Senior Citizens' Daycare Center**, West Bund, Shanghai, China

2014

Adaptation: Architecture and Change in China—an External Exhibition of La Biennale di Venezia, **Huaxin Business Center (Shanghai Google Creators' Society Center)**, Venice, Italy

2013

West Bund: A Biennial of Architecture and Contemporary Art, **Huaxin Business Center (Shanghai Google Creators' Society Center)**, Shanghai, China

Shenzhen Biannual, **Huaxin Business Center (Shanghai Google Creators' Society Center)**, Shenzhen, China

Zhu Xiaofeng's Works, School of Architecture and Urban Planning, Shenzhen University, Shenzhen, China

Museum of Contemporary Art Shanghai Exibition, **Dayu Artist Village and other works**, Museum of Contemporary Art, Shanghai, China

Eastern Promises—Contemporary Architecture and Spatial Practice in East Asia, **Jintao Village Community Pavilion**, MAK Museum, Vienna, Austria

| 2012 | China Design Exhibition, **Zhujiajiao Museum of Humanities and Arts and other works**, Shenzhen, China |

Triennial di Milano: From Research to Practice, **Zhujiajiao Museum of Humanities and Arts**, Milan, Italy

Hong Kong Biennale, **New Publicity: From East Bookstore**, Hong Kong, China

| 2011 | Chengdu Biennale Architecture Exhibition, **Elevated Multi-story Apt: A New Housing Prototype for Tomorrow**, Chengdu, China |

| 2010 | Venice Architecture Biennale—China Pavilion Architecture Exhibition, **Zhujiajiao Museum of Humanities and Arts**, Venice, Italy |

China Renewal, Zhengda Contemporary Museum, Shanghai, China

| 2009 | Shenzhen Hong Kong Biennale – Odyssey: Architecture and Literature, Shenzhen, China (curated by Ouning) |

Un-Natural, Cloudery, **Beijing Contemporary Art Center**, Beijing, China

My Moleskine 2009, **architects' sketches**, Shanghai, China

| 2008 | New Trends of Architecture in Europe and Asia Pacific 2008–2009, selected as one of the fifteen emerging architects in the EU and Asia Pacific regions; includes Tokyo, Lisbon, Istanbul, and Barcelona, among others (curated by Peter Cook and Toyo Ito) |

China Design Now, Victoria and Albert Museum, London, United Kingdom

Architopia: Works of 10 Architects from Shanghai and Beijing, **Green Pine Garden**, CIVA, Brussels, Belgium

| 2007 | Shenzhen Hong Kong Biennale, **New Socialist Workers' Apartment**, Shenzhen, China |

40 Under 40—Emerging Young Chinese Architects, Shanghai, China

Dasheng Exhibition, **The Lego Project**, Shanghai–Beijing–Guangzhou, China

| 2006 | China Contemporary Architecture, Netherlands Architecture Institute, Rotterdam, The Netherlands |

Yellow Box—Contemporary Art in Chinese Traditional Space, Xiao Xi Men, Shanghai, China

LECTURES

| 2021 | "Young Architects: Contemporary Locality," *The 19th Asian Congress of Architects*, Shanghai, China |

"Architects Meet School Principles," *Towards New Campus*, Shanghai, China

| 2020 | "Unbuilt," Guangzhou Design Week, Shanghai, China |

| 2019 | "The Renascence of Form-type: Chen Chi-kwan's Architectural Exploration at Tunghai University," *Craft Lecture Series*, Tongji University, Shanghai, China |

"Regeneration of Form-type: Selected Works of Scenic Architecture Office," *AIA International Region 2019 Conferenc*e, Shanghai, China

"Consistency and Renewal: 15 Years of Scenic Architecture Office," *Harvard Wisdom and China Practice Workshop*, Shanghai Library, Shanghai, China

| 2018 | "The Renaissance of Settlement and Form-type: An Architectural Reply to the Present Age," Faculty of Architecture, Hong Kong University, Hong Kong, China |

"Recent Works of Scenic Architecture Office," *Sino-Swiss Architecture Dialogue*, Shanghai, China

"Chen Chi-kwan's Architectural Exploration at Tunghai University 1954–1964," *Moving Away: Bauhaus in Asia Symposium*, China Design Museum, Hangzhou, Zhejiang, China

"Ontological Response," *International PhD Program Forum*, Tongji University, Shanghai, China

"Echo," The 25th Contemporary China Architecture Practice Forum, Suzhou, Jiangsu Province, China

"Echo: Regeneration of Settlement and Form-type," *35th Anniversary of Shenzhen University*, School of Architecture, Shenzhen, China

2017	"Dongyuan Qianxun Community Center," Dongyuan, Suzhou, Jiangsu Province, China
	"Ontological Response," School of Architecture, Xi'an Jiaotong-Liverpool University, Suzhou, Jiangsu Province, China
	"Pudong Adolescent Activity Center and Civic Art Center," *Shanghai Urban Space Art Season (SUSAS) Forum*, Shanghai, China
	"Process," *Lattice Book House Opening*, Shanghai, China
2016	"Ontological Response," *Contemporary Chinese Architecture Forum*, Harvard Graduate School of Design, Boston, United States
	"Architecture as the Extension of Human," Yantai University, Shandong Province, China
	"Architecture as the Extension of Human," Tongji University, Shanghai, China
	"Recent Works of Scenic Architecture Office," Hong Kong University Shanghai Study Center, Shanghai, China
2015	"Architecture as the Extension of Human Being," China Central Academy of Fine Arts (CAFA), Beijing, China
	"Architecture in Extension," Department of Architecture, Shanghai Jiaotong University, Shanghai, China
	"Renascence of Prototype—Chen Chi-kwan and His Architectural Explorations in Tunghai University," *"Let's Talk" segment at Shanghai City Art Festival*, Shanghai, China
	"Architecture Symbiotic with Nature," *Sino-Italy Academy Forum*, Florence, Italy
2014	"Cooperation with Nature," School of Architecture and Urban Planning, Nanjing University, Nanjing, China
	"Cooperation with Nature," *Architect @ Work Lecture*, Shanghai, China
	"Architecture as Medium," University of Florence, Florence, Italy
2013	"Suture Quality with Density," Hong Kong University of Shanghai Study Center, Shanghai, China
	"From Concept to Construction," Tongji University, Shanghai, China
	"Place: Time, Space and Matter," *Area Forum*, Shanghai, China
	"Cooperate with Nature," Shenzhen University, Shenzhen, China
2012	"Zhujiajiao Museum of Humanities and Arts," Rockbound Art Museum, Shanghai, China
	"What is Architecture Innovation For," *Architect @ Work Lecture*, Shanghai New International Expo Center (SNIEC), Shanghai, China
	"The Mission of Architecture," Museum of Contemporary Art Shanghai, Shanghai, China
2011	"A New Housing Typology for Future," *Qi Conference: Designing Aisa*, Singapore
	"Architecture as Media Between Human and Environment," College of Architecture and Urban Planning (graduate program), Tongji University, Shanghai, China
2010	"Reconstructing Scenery," School of Architecture and Urban Planning, Harbin Institute of Technology, Harbin, Heilongjiang Province, China
	"Works of Scenic Architecture Office 2004–2009," *Snowball Helsinki—Shanghai 2010, Finnish and Chinese Architecture Forum*, Shanghai, China
2009	"Practice for Contemporary China," College of Architecture and Urban Planning (graduate program), Tongji University, Shanghai, China
2008	"Scenic Architecture," *New Trends of Architecture in Europe and Asia-Pacific Exhibition*, Tokyo, Japan
	"Recent Works," *Architopia Exhibition*, CIVA, Brussels, Belgium
2007	"Three Sceneries," *Vanke Art and Environment Committee Lecture*, Hangzhou, Zhejiang, China

PUBLICATIONS

Books

2021 Zhu Xiaofeng, *The Rebirth of Form-type* (Shanghai: Tongji University Press, 2021)

Chris van Uffelen, *China: The New Creative Power in Architecture* (Salenstein: Braun Publishing AG, 2021)

2020 Kenneth Frampton, *Modern Architecture, A Critical History*, 5th ed. (London: Thames & Hudson, 2020)

2019 Jiang Limin and Liu Ling, eds., for Tongji Architectural Design (Group) Co. Ltd, *New Era Basic Education Building Design Guidelines* (Beijing: China Architecture and Building Press, 2019)

2018 Li Xiangning, ed., *Towards a Critical Pragmatism: Contemporary Architecture in China* , trans., He Yanfei (Guangxi: Guangxi Normal University Press, 2018)

Helen Thomas, *Drawing Architecture* (London: Phaidon, 2018)

Feng Qiong and Liu Jingrui, eds., *New Architecture in Shanghai* (Guangxi: Guangxi Normal University Press, 2018)

2017 Zhu Xiaofeng, "Common and Timeless Spaces" in *The Social Imperative—Architecture and the City in China*, ed., H. Koon Wee (Taipei: Actar, 2017)

2015 Archipelago, *Conversations Among Architects* (Shanghai: Tongji University Press, 2015)

Paul Jackson, *Complete Pleats: Pleating Techniques for Fashion, Architecture and Design* (London: Laurence King Publishing, 2015)

Zhu Xiaofeng, "Origin and Evolution," in *New Observation: Architectural Criticism*, ed., Shi Jian (Shanghai: Tongji University Press, 2015)

2014 Ruan Qingyue, *Next Skyline: Contemporary Architecture Designed by Chinese* (Beijing: Publishing House of Electronics Industry, 2014)

Zhu Xiaofeng, "Dialogue with Nature," in *China Environmental Art Design Yearbook 05*, ed., Bao Shidu (Beijing: China Architecture and Building Press, 2014)

2013 Zhi Wenjun and Xu Jie, eds., *Chinese Contemporary Architecture 2008–2012* (Shanghai: Tongji University Press, 2013)

2011 Ioanni Delsante, ed., *Experimental Architecture in Shanghai* (Rome: Officina Edizioni, 2011)

Designer and Designing Magazine, ed., *New Cultural Architecture in China* (Tianjing: Tianjing University Press, 2011)

2010 Tang Keyang, ed., *Meeting China Here: The China Pavilion at the 12th Venice Architecture Biennale* (Beijing: New Star Press, 2010)

Ou Ning, ed., *Wandering: Architectural Experience and Literary Imationation* (Beijing: China Youth Press, 2010)

Ge Lili, Han Jiawen, and Lun Jiyun, eds., *Cases of Avant-garde Architecture* (Beijing: New Star Press, 2010)

2009 Zheng Shiling, ed., *New China, New Architecture: 60 Architects in 60 Years* (Jiangxi: Jiangxi Science and Technology Press, 2009)

Sun Tian and Bu Bing, *Un-Natural* (Beijing: Beijing Center for the Arts Press, 2009)

Xu Jie and Zhi Wenjun, eds., *Building China: Top 48 Contemporary Chinese Architectural Design Institutes and Their Works (2006–2008)* (Shenyang: Liaoning Science and Technology Publishing House, 2009)

2008 Phaidon Press, ed., *The Phaidon Atlas of 21st Century World Architecture* (Phaidon Press, 2008)

2006 Philip Jodidio, ed., *Architecture in China* (Taschen, 2006)

Yu Bing, ed., *Domus 78 + Chinese Architects and Designers* (Beijing: China Architecture and Building Press, 2006)

Xu Jie and Zhi Wenjun, eds., *Building China: Top Forty Contemporary Architects Firms in China* (Shenyang: Liaoning Science and Technology Publishing House, 2006)

Magazines/Journals

2021 Zhu Xiaofeng, "Superimposed Construction: An Art Gallery on Market," *Architecture Technique*, 27, no. 10 (Oct. 2021): 11–22

Zhu Xiaofeng, "Art Gallery on Market," *Contemporary Architecture*, no. 10 (Oct. 2021): 92–99

Jiang Jiawei, "Xitang Art Gallery on Market: Steel and Wood Integrated Structure Design and Exploration, of Home Form-type," *Time + Architecture*, no. 10 (Sep. 2021): 76–83

2020 Scenic Architecture Office, "Expo Village," *Architecture China* Vol. 2, Winter Edition, 2020, 102

Zhu Xiaofeng, "Inspiration of Order: The Educational Space of the Huazhan Campus of No. 1 Elementary School on Gao'an Road, Shanghai," *Architectural Journal*, no. 6 (Dec. 2020): 28–37

2019 Zhu Xiaofeng and Jiang Meng, "Extension of Homes: Design Concept of the Activity Houses on Yunjin Road," *Time + Architecture*, no. 6 (Nov. 2019): 80–89

Scenic Architecture Office, "Community Center in Suzhou," *Detail*, July 2019, 42

Qing Feng and Zhu Xiaofeng, "The Formation of Settlements: A Dialogue with Zhu Xiaofeng, the Founder of Scenic Architecture Office," *The Architect*, no. 2 (April 2019): 114–122

Scenic Architecture Office, "Deep Dive Rowing Club," *Architectural Journal*, no. 1 (Jan. 2019): 80–83

Du Jie, "In Between Nature: Deep Dive Rowing Club," *Architectural Journal*, no. 1 (Jan. 2019): 84–87

Zhu Xiaofeng, Du Jie, and Zhou Yan, "Deep Dive Rowing Club, Shanghai, China," *World Architecture*, no. 1 (Jan. 2019): 70

Zhu Xiaofeng, "Form-type Drive in Urban Renewal: Homes for Public Life in the Runway Park," *Time + Architecture*, no. 4 (April 2019): 50–54

2018 Ye Jingxian, "Caring for Nature in Prefabrication Construction: Shanghai Century Park—Deep Dive Rowing Club by Scenic Architecture," *Time + Architecture*, no. 6 (Nov. 2018): 86–91

Zhu Xiaofeng, "Garden and Architecture," *Time + Architecture*, no. 4 (July 2018): 51

2017 Zhu Xiaofeng, "The Archetypal Role on the Design of Lattice Book House," *Architectural Journal*, no. 10 (Oct. 2017): 87–89

Zhu Xiaofeng and Liang Shan, "Lattice Book House," *Architectural Journal*, no. 10 (Oct. 2017): 82–86

Dai Chun, "A Place's Time: Community Centre at the Dongyuan Qianxun Complex, Interview with Zhu Xiaofeng, Design Principal of Scenic Architecture," *Time + Architecture*, no. 4 (July 2017): 134–139

Li Xiangning, "Scenic Architecture Office: From Landscape to the Ontology of Architecture, Letter from China," *The Plan*, Oct. 2017, 46

Scenic Architecture Office, "Dongyuan Qianxun Community Center," *C3 Magazine Special: Contemporary Communities* (Korea: C3 Magazine), 186

2016 Zhang Bin, Zhu Xiaofeng, Chen Yifeng, and Liu Yichun, "A Breakthrough of Restrictions: A Quadrilateral Conversation on the Design of Kindergartens and Elementary Schools," *Architectural Journal*, no. 4 (April 2016): 96–103

Zhu Xiaofeng, "Childhood in Honeycomb, East China Normal University Affiliated Bilingual Kindergarten, Shanghai," *Time + Architecture*, no. 3 (May 2016): 90–97

2015 Zhu Xiaofeng, "Shengli Street Neighborhood Committee and Elderly Daycare Center at Zhujiajiao, Shanghai, China," *World Architecture*, no. 11 (Nov. 2015): 50–55

Zhu Xiaofeng, "Huaxin Business Center: Floating Courtyards," *Trends*, Nov. 2015

Zhu Xiaofeng, "Renascence of Prototype: Chen Chi-kwan and His Architectural Explorations in Tunghai University," *Architectural Journal*, no.1 (Jan. 2015): 74–81

Lo Shi-Wei and Zhu Xiaofeng, "A Conversation on the Early Architecture at Tunghai University," *Architectural Journal*, no. 1 (Jan. 2015): 82–83

2014 Zhu Xiaofeng, "Huaxin Business Center," *Area Magazine*, Oct. 2014

Gong Weimin, "Localized Architecture: Zhu Xiaofeng and His Works," *World Architecture Review*, no. 1 (Jan. 2014): 12–13

Zhu Xiaofeng, "To Illuminate the Meaning of Landscape with an Active Heart," *Pro Design*, March 2014

Zhu Xiaofeng, "Origins and Evolution," *World Architecture Review*, no. 1 (Jan. 2014): 7–11

2013   Zhu Xiaofeng and Xiaomai, "Landscape in the Scenery, Zhujiajiao Humanities and Arts Museum," *id+c*, no. 12 (Dec. 2013): 103–108

Zhu Xiaofeng, "With the Law of Nature, Huaxin Business Center in Shanghai," *id+c*, no. 12 (Dec. 2013): 102–107

Scenic Architecture Office, "Huaxin Exhibition Center," *Urban Environment Design*, no. 12 (Dec. 2013): 216–223

Guo Yiming and Zhu Xiaofeng, "Between Abstraction and Concretion Structure and Space of Huaxin Center," *Architectural Journal*, no. 11 (Nov. 2013): 42–53

Zhu Xiaofeng, "Dialogue with Nature," *Architecture and Art*, Nov. 2013

Zhu Xiaofeng, "Huaxin Exhibition Center," *First Impression*, Nov. 2013

Zhu Xiaofeng, "Intergrowth with Tree," *Casa Da Abitare*, Nov. 2013

Zeng Zeng, "Dialogue with Nature," *Architecture and Art*, Nov. 2013

Scenic Architecture Office, "Huaxin Business Center, Shanghai, China," *Urbanism and Architecture*, no. 23 (Oct. 2013): 70–77

Zhu Xiaofeng and Ge Lili, "Collaborate with Nature: Design Notion Behind the Huaxin Business Center," *Spaces*, Sep. 2013

Zhu Xiaofeng, "Huaxin Business Center," *Detail*, Sep. 2013

Zhu Xiaofeng, "Recreation Room for Villagers in Jintao Village," *La Vie*, March 2013

Zhu Xiaofeng, "Wandering in the Garden: From East Bookstore," *Spaces*, March 2013

Zhu Xiaofeng, "Public Facility in Jiading Ziqidonglai Park," *Di*, Feb. 2013

Zhu Xiaofeng, "Recreation Room for Villagers in Jintao Village," *Architectural Journal*, no. 1 (Jan. 2013): 60–67

2012   Zhu Xiaofeng and Iwan Baan, "Zhujiajiao Museum of Humanities and Arts, Shanghai, China," *World Architecture*, no. 12 (Dec. 2012): 78–81

Scenic Architecture Office, "Special Edition for Works of Scenic Architecture Office," *New Architecture*, no. 6 (Nov. 2012)

Scenic Architecture Office, "Shengli Street Neighborhood Committee and Senior Citizens' Daycare Center," *Urban Environment Design*, no. 8 (Aug. 2012): 238–244

Liu Yichun, Chen Yifeng, and Zhu Xiaofeng, "An Abstract Urban Scenario," *Domus* (Chinese edition), Aug. 2012

Zhu Xiaofeng, "Architecture as Media Between Human and Environment: Five Buildings by Scenic Architecture," *Time + Architecture*, no. 1 (Jan. 2012): 62–67

Zhu Xiaofeng, "Community Pavilion at Jintao Village," *Architecture and Art*, Nov. 2012

Zhu Xiaofeng, "From East Bookstore," *In Out*, June 2012

Dong Xuan, "Ziqidonglai—a Propitious Omen," *Architecture and Art*, June 2012

Zhu Xiaofeng, "Zhujiajiao Museum of Humanities and Arts," *Trendshome*, June 2012

Li Difei, "Walls and Silhouettes," *Casa Da Abitare*, April 2012

Dong Xuan, "Variation and Rhythm: Jumping Notes," *Architecture and Art*, April 2012

Zhu Xiaofeng, "Zhujiajiao Museum of Humanities and Arts," *Urbanism and Architecture*, no. 7 (March 2012): 74–80

Zhu Xiaofeng, "From East Bookstore," *Urbanism and Architecture*, no.6 (March 2012): 72–76

Zhang You, ed., "New Story at the River Fork," *Architecture and Art*, March 2012

Li Wei, "Thinking Endlessly," *Interior Designer*, March 2012

Zhu Xiaofeng, "From East Bookstore," *Living*, Feb. 2012

Zhu Xiaofeng, "Vanke Holiday Town Community Center," *Architecture Knowledge*, Feb. 2012

Zhang Dou, "Dancing in the Woods: A Review of the Design of Jiading New Town Ziqidonglai Park, Shanghai," *Time + Architecture*, no. 1 (Jan. 2012): 52–57

2011 Li Zheng, "Dating with the Old Tree: Zhujiajiao Museum of Humanities and Arts," *Interior Design*, Oct. 2011

Zhu Xiaofeng, "Zhujiajiao Museum of Humanities and Arts," *Spaces (Korea)*, Aug. 2011

Zhu Xiaofeng, Lili, and Iwan Baan, "New Landmark in Zhujiajiao Town," *Spaces*, June 2011, 94

Li Difei, "Community Pavilion in New Village," *Casa Da Abitare*, June 2011

Zhu Xiaofeng, "Architectural Savour of Zhujiajiao Museum of Humanities and Arts," *Urban Environment Design*, no. 5 (May 2011): 276–281

Ru Lei, "Wonder in Frames: Zhujiajiao Museum of Humanities and Arts," *Domus (Chinese edition)*, May 2011

Song Yang, "Flexible Language of Spaces: Community Pavilion at Jintao Village," *Mark (Chinese edition)*, March 2011

Dai Chun, "Insertion: Zhujiajiao Museum of Humanities and Arts Designed by Scenic Architecture," *Time + Architecture*, no.6 (Jan. 2011): 96–103

Zhu Xiaofeng, "Raised Multi-storey Apartments: A Housing Prototype for Future New Towns," *Time + Architecture*, no. 5 (Sep. 2011): 80–81

2010 Zhu Xiaofeng, "Zhujiajiao Museum of Humanities and Arts," *Interior Designer*, Dec. 2010

Zhu Xiaofeng, "Dashawan Beach Facility at Lianyungang," *Interior Designer*, Dec. 2010

Zhu Xiaofeng, "Reconstructing the Scenery: Dashawan Beach Facility at Lianyungang, Jiangsu Province," *Time + Architecture*, no. 3 (March 2010): 88–93

Zhu Xiaofeng, "Zhujiajiao Museum of Humanities and Arts," *Area*, Feb. 2010

Song Baolin, "New Architecture in Old Town: Zhujiajiao Museum of Humanities and Arts," *Di*, Feb. 2010

2008 Scenic Architecture Office, " 'Wind and Fire Wheels' in Chinese Architecture," *IW*, Oct. 2008

Zhuang Shen, "Harmony and Variety—Vanke Holiday Town Community Center Designed by Scenic Architecture Office," *Time + Architecture*, no. 3 (March 2008): 88–93

2007 Zhu Xiaofeng, "SuZhou Museum—The Duet of New Chinese Garden and Monumentality," *World Architecture*, no. 4 (April 2007): 118

Zhu Xiaofeng, "To Keep and To Discard: A Critique on the Architectural Conception of Xiayu Kindergarten," *World Architecture*, no. 2 (Feb. 2007): 35–37

2006 Zhu Xiaofeng, "An Attitude of Appropriateness: 'One Design' Strategy on Zhejiang University Wang Xin Science Park Project," *Time + Architecture*, no. 3 (May 2006): 108–113

2005 Liu Yu-yang, "The Familiar and Unfamiliar Scenery: On Works of Zhu Xiaofeng," *Time + Architecture*, no. 6 (Nov. 2005): 42–49

2003 Zhu Xiaofeng, "The Logic of Choice—New York MOMA's Expansion," *World Architecture*, no. 4 (May 2003): 94–97

1998 Zhu Xiaofeng, "Design Process on Shenzhen University Student Center," *Architectural Journal*, no. 2 (Feb. 1998): 31–34

STAFF APPRECIATION

In the past eighteen years that Scenic Architecture Office has been established, we have crossed many milestones and attained many proud successes. Our continuous development and perseverance toward progress is a result of the determined and united effort of our devoted team. We take this opportunity to express our gratitude to everyone for their hard work, and to also thank our partners whom we have collaborated with on this journey.

Employees

Current Staff

Zhu Xiaofeng	He Beifei	Geng Yuntong
Li Qitong	Zhu Xiaoye	Sun Jianong
Zhuang Xinjia	Shen Ziwei	Chen Xuanxiang
Jiang Meng	Wang Junyuan	Bian Suqi
Zhou Yan	Zhang Chi	Su Kaiqiang
Pi Liming	Lin Xiaosheng	LiuYunong
Zhang Xuan	Song Yixuan	Wang Yimin
Chen Chingwen	Su Kaiqiang	Liang Xin

Former Staff

Xu Lei	Li Wenjia	Ye Lizhou
Cai Jiangsi	Xu Ye	Zhang Guohao
Ding Penghua	Sheng Tai	Ye Guiying
Du Jie	Cai Mian	Xu Linfeng
Pablo Gonzalez Riera	Shi Yan'an	He Jing
Liang Shan	Yang Taohui	Guo Yanling
Guo Dan	Xu Xiwen	Hu Bo
Li Shuo	Hu Qiming	Shi Tao
Shi Yin	Shan Haidong	Song Yikun
Zhou Wei	He Yong	Xia Chao
Pei Yu	Wu Jian	Zhang Tianyu
Chen Tianle	Zhang Hao	Gao Min
Guo Zhenxin	Dong Zhiping	Wang Song
Ding Xufen	Li Guangyao	Xi Yu
Su Shenliang	Hu Xianmei	Jin Bo
Du Shigang	Gao Zhenzheng	Zheng Junmu
Yang Hong	Lin Wenming	Su Wushun

Interns

Yan Jun, Li Jiajia, Yang Xuan, Gu Liwen, Huang Longchang, Liu Linxue, Wang Yixiu, Dong Dawei, Xu Yingjie, Yu Mengjun, Wu Zhiyang, Zhou Huaqiu, Wang Yu, Mei Fupeng, Feng Feifei, Wu Pan, Du Mili, Sun Najia, Liu Chenjun, Zhou Guyang, Chen Jun, Liang Xinting, Li Haoran, Zhang Heyi, Guo Ying, Lv Shun, Jia Chengyue, Wang Lu, Cheng Yuxi, Ettore Santi, Jin Chuhao, Zhang Pingting, Zhou Zhou, Li Jianbo, Yang Ningqiu, Zhao Yue, Jiang Meng, Li Zhejian, Dai Qiaoqi, Tang Yun, Hu Jialin, Qi Rudan, Wu Shurui, Zhou Yitong, Ru Kai, Qu You, Yang Rong, Li Yadong, Yan Shuang, Zhu Xudong, Zhang Ji, Li Zhenshen, Meng Xing, Zhao Jingrong, Sun Xingyuan, Xie Tao, Li Hao, Deng Qianxin, Li Yuqian, Wang Han, Luo Qi, Fu Rong, Su Zhenqiang, Xiao Zaiyuan, Shang Yunpeng, Li Cheng, Liu Tong, Yan Shuang, Weng Wenqian, Ye Chenhui, Zou Zhile, Lv Xintian, Lei Chang, Zhu Jingdan, Feng Lingsheng, Zheng Jing, He Ye, Fu Zihui, Yan Wenzheng, Liu Peibin, Song Yunfan, Zhang Yu, Zhang Yinxian, Sha Chengjun, Zhu Qiqi, Bu Xianhui, Gan Yunni, Huang Hanxin, Lv Haihan, Jiao Lei, Song Xiaoyue, Yang Zixuan, He Ran, Sun Haopeng, Qi Aofei, Wen Meihui, Zhao Ling, Huang Chunling, Gao Chenyang, Xu Jingyi, Ma Ziqiao, Shi Shuaibo, Yu Yulin, Fillipa Wang, Li Xuan, Zhang Han, He Wenxing, Hou Pengfei, Tao Keyu, Zhao Dan, Wang Mingzhen, Hu Siyuan, Zhou Yan, Ning Liteng, Fang Shiyu, Chen Xiafei, Zeng Jing, Lai Siyu, Yu Siya, Shang Yutao, Chen Sini, Li Jing, Li Ying, Qu Xin, Sun Ying, Song Mingjie, Jiang Zaijie, Huo Yanlong, Chen Yujin, Lin Ying, Chen Xi, Xu Youlu, Lu Sihan, Hu Chenghai

IMAGE CREDITS

All images and illustrations are courtesy of Scenic Architecture Office, other than the exceptions listed here:

Jeremy Chen: 30–34, 36–41

Su Shengliang (Schran Image Studio): 35, 118–127, 136–151, 162–179, 208–211, 216–220, 221 (bottom), 222, 252–263, 274–289

Iwan Baan: 50–62, 64–65

Zhu Xiaofeng: 63, 212, 221 (top), 223

Liang Shan: 74–85, 213–215

Zhu Runzi: 96–109, 232–241

Shen Zhonghai: 188–197

Dongyuan Design: 250–251, 262–263, cover

Published in Australia in 2022 by
The Images Publishing Group Pty Ltd
ABN 89 059 734 431

Offices

Melbourne
Waterman Business Centre
Suite 64, Level 2 UL40
1341 Dandenong Rd, Chadstone,
Victoria 3148
Australia
Tel: +61 3 8564 8122

New York
6 West 18th Street 4B
New York, NY 10011
United States
Tel: +1 212 645 1111

Shanghai
6F, Building C, 838 Guangji Road
Hongkou District, Shanghai 200434
China
Tel: +86 021 31260822

books@imagespublishing.com
www.imagespublishing.com

Copyright © Authors and photographers as indicated 2022
The Images Publishing Group Reference Number: 1581

All rights reserved. Apart from any fair dealing for the purposes of private study, research, criticism or review as permitted under the Copyright Act, no part of this publication may be reproduced, stored in a retrieval system, or transmitted in any form by any means, electronic, mechanical, photocopying, recording or otherwise, without the written permission of the publisher.

A catalogue record for this book is available from the National Library of Australia

Title: Rebirth of Form-type: Selected Works of Scenic Architecture Office
Author: Zhu Xiaofeng (Ed.)
ISBN: 9781864708882

Printed by Toppan Excel (Dongguan) Printing CO,. LTD., in Hong Kong/China

IMAGES has included on its website a page for special notices in relation to this and its other publications. Please visit www.imagespublishing.com

Every effort has been made to trace the original source of copyright material contained in this book. The publishers would be pleased to hear from copyright holders to rectify any errors or omissions.

The information and illustrations in this publication have been prepared and supplied by Zhu Xiaofeng and Scenic Architecture Office. While all reasonable efforts have been made to ensure accuracy, the publishers do not, under any circumstances, accept responsibility for errors, omissions, and representations, express or implied.